FIX-IT and FORGET-IT®
COOKING FOR TWO

150 SMALL-BATCH SLOW COOKER RECIPES

HOPE COMERFORD

Good Books

New York, New York

10 9

Library of Congress Cataloging-in-Publication Data is available on file.

Cover design by Jane Sheppard
Cover photo by Bonnie Matthews

Print ISBN: 978-1-68099-312-7
Ebook ISBN: 978-1-68099-314-1

Printed in China

In loving Memory of Lori Stull.

"Because someone we love is in heaven, there is a bit of heaven in our home."

Table of Contents

Welcome to Fix-It and Forget-It Cooking for Two

Do you ever find yourself frustrated because all the recipes you make leave you with leftovers for days? If so, this book is just what you're looking for! We've compiled 150 down-to-earth, tasty, and easy recipes designed specifically for two. That's right! All of the recipes in this book will make just 2–4 servings. Whether you're cooking for your spouse, significant other, partner, friend, sibling, parents, neighbors, etc., we're providing you with breakfasts, appetizers and snacks, soups, stews and chilis, main dishes, side dishes and vegetables, desserts, and beverages all perfectly portioned for two (sometimes with just enough for a second helping or leftovers for tomorrow's lunch!).

When I was living by myself as a college student, I had a small 2-qt. slow cooker and spent a lot of time figuring out how to pare down recipes I would find so I didn't have leftovers for an entire week. I certainly didn't have the freezer space to freeze anything, so more than a day or two of leftovers wasn't an option. I didn't like wasting food and I didn't have a neighbor I could bring leftovers to.

I hear stories like mine from so many people! We've heard your voices and your wish has finally come true. We certainly hope you enjoy these amazing recipes for two!

Choosing a Slow Cooker

What Size Slow Cooker Do I Need for This Book?

Each recipe in this book is designed for a 1½–3-qt. slow cooker. If you use a bigger slow cooker, you will most likely not get the results you're looking for. Slow cookers are meant to be ⅔ to ¾ full in order to cook properly. Since these recipes are meant for two, you'll be making smaller batches than you might be used to. It's important to use the correct size slow cooker.

Get to Know Your Slow Cooker . . .

Plan a little time to get acquainted with your slow cooker. Each slow cooker has its own personality—just like your oven (and your car). Plus, many new slow cookers cook hotter and faster than earlier models. I think that with all of the concern for food safety, the slow cooker manufacturers have amped up their settings so that "High," "Low," and "Warm" are all higher temperatures than in the older models. That means they cook hotter—and therefore, faster—than the first slow cookers. The beauty of these little machines is that they're supposed to cook low and slow. We count on that when we flip the switch in the morning before we leave the house for ten hours or so. So, because none of us knows what kind of temperament our slow cooker has until we try it out, nor how hot it cooks—don't assume anything. Save yourself a disappointment and make the first recipe in your new slow cooker on a day when you're at home. Cook it for the shortest amount of time the recipe calls for. Then, check the food to see if it's done. Or if you start smelling food that seems to be finished, turn off the cooker and rescue your food.

Also, all slow cookers seem to have a "hot spot," which is of great importance to know, especially when baking with your slow cooker. This spot may tend to burn food in that area if you're not careful. If you're baking directly in your slow cooker, I recommend covering the "hot spot" with some foil.

Take Notes . . .

Don't be afraid to make notes in your cookbook. It's yours! Chances are, it will eventually get passed down to someone in your family and they will love and appreciate all of your musings. Take note of which slow cooker you used and exactly how long it took to cook the recipe. The next time you make it, you won't need to try to remember. Apply what you learned to the next recipes you make in your cooker. If another recipe says it needs to cook 7–9 hours, and you've discovered your slow cooker cooks on the faster side, cook that recipe for 6–6½ hours and then check it. You can always cook a recipe longer—but you can't reverse things if it's overdone.

Get Creative . . .

If you know your morning is going to be hectic, prepare everything the night before, take it out so the crock warms up to room temperature when you first get up in the morning, then plug it in and turn it on as you're leaving the house.

If you want to make something that has a short cook time and you're going to be gone longer than that, cook it the night before and refrigerate it for the next day. Warm it up when you get home. Or, cook those recipes on the weekend when you know you'll be home and eat them later in the week.

Slow-Cooking Tips and Tricks and Other Things You May Not Know

- As mentioned above, slow cookers tend to work best when they're ⅔ to ¾ of the way full. You may need to increase the cooking time if you've exceeded that amount, or reduce it if you've put in less than that.
- Keep your veggies on the bottom. That puts them in more direct contact with the heat. The fuller your slow cooker, the longer it will take its contents to cook. Also, the more

densely packed the cooker's contents are, the longer they will take to cook. And finally, the larger the chunks of meat or vegetables, the more time they will need to cook.

- Keep the lid on! Every time you take a peek, you lose 20 minutes of cooking time. Please take this into consideration each time you lift the lid! I know, some of you can't help yourself and are going to lift anyway. Just don't forget to tack on 20 minutes to your cook time for each time you peeked!

- Sometimes it's beneficial to remove the lid. If you'd like your dish to thicken a bit, take the lid off during the last half hour to hour of cooking time.

- The outside of your slow cooker will be hot! Please remember to keep it out of reach of children and keep that in mind for yourself as well!

- Get yourself a quick-read meat thermometer and use it! This helps remove the question of whether or not your meat is fully cooked, and helps prevent you from overcooking your meat as well.
  - Internal Cooking Temperatures: Beef—125–130°F (rare); 140–145°F (medium); 160°F (well-done)
  - Pork—140–145°F (rare); 145–150°F (medium); 160°F (well-done)
  - Turkey and Chicken—165°F
  - Frozen Meat: The basic rule of thumb is, don't put frozen meat into the slow cooker. The meat does not reach the proper internal temperature in time. This especially applies to thick cuts of meat! Proceed with caution!

- Add fresh herbs 10 minutes before the end of the cooking time to maximize their flavor.

- If your recipe calls for cooked pasta, add it 10 minutes before the end of the cooking time if the cooker is on High; 30 minutes before the end of the cooking time if it's on Low. Then the pasta won't get mushy.

- If your recipe calls for sour cream or cream, stir it in 5 minutes before the end of the cooking time. You want it to heat but not boil or simmer.

- Approximate Slow Cooker Temperatures (Remember, each slow cooker is different):
  - High—212°F–300°F
  - Low—170°F–200°F
  - Simmer—185°F
  - Warm—165°F

- Cooked beans freeze well. Store them in freezer bags (squeeze the air out first) or freezer boxes. Cooked and dried bean measurements:
  - 16-oz. can, drained = about 1¾ cups beans
  - 19-oz. can, drained = about 2 cups beans
  - 1 lb. dried beans (about 2½ cups) = 5 cups cooked beans

Breakfasts

Maple Sausage Breakfast Bake

Hope Comerford, Clinton Township, MI

Prep. Time: 15 minutes ⚄ Cooking Time: 3–3½ hours ⚄ Ideal slow-cooker size: 2-qt.

3 eggs

½ cup gluten-free or regular baking mix

½ cup shredded Colby jack cheese

1 cup milk

¼ tsp. salt

⅛ tsp. pepper

6 maple flavored gluten-free or regular sausage links, browned, chopped

¼ cup diced onion

maple syrup, *optional*

1. Spray the crock with nonstick spray.

2. In a bowl, mix together the eggs, baking mix, shredded cheese, milk, salt, and pepper. Stir in the sausage and onion. Spread this mixture out evenly over the bottom of the crock.

3. Cover and cook on Low for 3–3½ hours.

4. Serve with maple syrup drizzled over the top, if desired.

Divided into 2 portions, made with regular baking mix, before adding syrup, each portion contains:

Calories: 505
Fat: 38g
Sodium: 1655mg
Carbs: 49g
Sugar: 10g
Protein: 32g

- Gluten-Free
- Soy-Free
- Nut-Free

Sunday Breakfast Sausage Casserole

Sue Smith, Saginaw, MI

Prep. Time: 15 minutes ⚶ Cooking Time: 1–2 hours ⚶ Ideal slow-cooker size: 2-qt.

2 cups cubed day-old bread

I cup shredded sharp cheddar cheese

12-oz. can evaporated milk

5 eggs, slightly beaten

½ tsp. dry mustard

¼ tsp. onion powder

fresh ground pepper, to taste

8-oz. pkg. pork sausage, cooked, crumbled, and drained

1. Place bread in greased slow cooker.

2. Sprinkle with the cheese.

3. Combine the milk, eggs, dry mustard, onion powder, and pepper in a medium bowl.

4. Pour evenly over bread and cheese.

5. Sprinkle with the sausage.

6. Cover with the lid and refrigerate overnight.

7. Cover and cook on High for 1 hour or Low for 2, or until done.

NOTE
This recipe makes enough for seconds or leftovers!

Makes 4 servings. Each portion contains:

Calories: 519

Fat: 36g

Sodium: 765mg

Carbs: 20g

Sugar: 11g

Protein: 31g

• Nut-Free

Laurie's Breakfast Casserole

Sue Smith, Saginaw, MI

Prep. Time: 25 minutes   ⚬   *Cooking Time: 3 hours*   ⚬   *Ideal slow-cooker size: 3-qt.*

½ cup rice, cooked with 1 cup water

4 oz. cottage cheese

½ pkg. (about 5 oz.) frozen spinach, thawed and squeezed dry

½ lb. sausage, cooked and drained

5 eggs, beaten, *divided*

½ cup mushrooms

¼ cup Parmesan cheese, *divided*

1. Mix together the cooked rice, cottage cheese, spinach, cooked sausage, 3 beaten eggs, and mushrooms.

2. Sprinkle 2 tablespoons Parmesan cheese on the bottom of a greased slow cooker. Pour in the rice mixture.

3. Pour remaining beaten eggs over the top.

4. Sprinkle 2 tablespoons Parmesan cheese on top.

5. Cover and cook on High for 3 hours or until a knife comes out clean after being inserted in the center.

Serving suggestion:

Serve with fresh fruit.

Makes 3 servings (one of you will want seconds!).
Each serving contains:

Calories: 500
Fat: 28g
Sodium: 938mg
Carbs: 30g
Sugar: 2g
Protein: 23g

- Gluten-Free
- Nut-Free

Bring-on-the-Bacon Brunch

Hope Comerford, Clinton Township, MI

Prep. Time: 15 minutes ⚬ *Cooking Time: 2–3 hours* ⚬ *Ideal slow-cooker size: 2-qt.*

5 oz. Brussels sprouts, thinly sliced

4 slices bacon, cooked, chopped

¼ cup shredded Swiss cheese

½ cup sour cream

½ cup low-fat cottage cheese

¼ cup gluten-free or regular baking mix

2 Tbsp. butter, melted

1 egg

1. Spray crock with nonstick spray.

2. Spread the Brussels sprouts out evenly across the bottom of the crock. Sprinkle the bacon evenly across the top, followed by the Swiss cheese.

3. In a blender or food processor, blend together the sour cream, cottage cheese, baking mix, butter, and egg until smooth. Pour this mixture over the contents in the crock.

4. Cover and cook on Low for 2–3 hours.

Makes 2 servings. Each serving contains:

Calories: 510
Fat: 33g
Sodium: 733mg
Carbs: 20g
Sugar: 4g
Protein: 21g

- Gluten-Free
- Soy-Free
- Nut-Free

Breakfast-in-a-Crock

Hope Comerford, Clinton Township, MI

Prep. Time: 15 minutes ⚬ *Cooking Time: 3–4 hours* ⚬ *Ideal slow-cooker size: 2-qt.*

1 ½ cups shredded gluten-free or regular frozen hash browns

½ cup diced cooked ham

¼ cup diced onion

½ cup shredded cheddar cheese

4 eggs

2 Tbsp. milk

¼ tsp. salt

¼ tsp. onion powder

¼ tsp. garlic powder

dash of hot sauce

1. Spray crock with nonstick spray.

2. Spread the hash browns evenly across the bottom of the crock, followed by a layer of the ham, then the onion, then the cheese.

3. In a bowl, whisk together the eggs, milk, salt, onion powder, garlic powder, and dash of hot sauce. Pour this over the contents of the crock.

4. Cover and cook on Low for 3–4 hours.

Makes 2 servings. Each serving contains:

Calories: 467
Fat: 26g
Sodium: 723mg
Carbs: 26g
Sugar: 1g
Protein: 30g

- Gluten-Free
- Soy-Free
- Nut-Free

Ham and Swiss Breakfast Casserole

Hope Comerford, Clinton Township, MI

Prep. Time: 15 minutes ⚘ *Cooking Time: 3–4 hours* ⚘ *Ideal slow-cooker size: 2-qt.*

5 slices gluten-free bread or 3–4 slices regular bread, crust trimmed off

1 cup shredded Swiss cheese

½ cup cooked ham, chopped

¼ cup chopped onion

3 eggs

½ cup unsweetened almond milk

½ tsp. salt

¼ tsp. dried dill

¼ tsp. dried parsley

⅛ tsp. pepper

dash of hot sauce

1. Line the crock with parchment paper.

2. Press the bread into the bottom of the crock and up the sides about 1 inch to form a crust.

3. Sprinkle the Swiss cheese, ham, and onion evenly over the crust.

4. In a bowl, whisk together the eggs, almond milk, salt, dill, parsley, pepper, and hot sauce. Pour over the contents of the crock.

5. Cover and cook on Low for 3–4 hours, or until a knife comes out clean from the center.

Makes 2 servings. Using gluten-free bread, each serving contains:

Calories: 615
Fat: 30g
Sodium: 1228mg
Carbs: 36g
Sugar: 5g
Protein: 38g

- Gluten-Free
- Soy-Free
- Nut-Free

Southwest Breakfast Burritos

MarJanita Geigley, Lancaster, PA

Prep. Time: 30 minutes ⚶ *Cooking Time: 2 hours* ⚶ *Ideal slow-cooker size: 3-qt.*

¼ lb. bulk sausage, browned and drained

1 chopped green pepper

¼ cup chopped onion

1 Tbsp. melted butter

4 scrambled eggs

¼ tsp. salt

⅛ tsp. pepper

¼ tsp. chives

¼ tsp. cilantro

1 cup shredded cheddar cheese

flour tortillas

salsa

1. Mix all ingredients except flour tortillas and salsa.

2. Place mixture inside flour tortillas and roll up in burrito style.

3. Lay in a greased crock. Cook on Low for 2 hours.

4. Serve warm and topped with salsa.

Makes 2 servings. With 2 flour tortillas, cheese, and plain scrambled eggs, each serving contains:

Calories: 676
Fat: 48g
Sodium: 1083mg
Carbs: 21g
Sugar: 4g
Protein: 37g

• Nut-Free

Southwest Quiche

Hope Comerford, Clinton Township, MI

Prep. Time: 15 minutes ⚜ Cooking Time: 3–4 hours ⚜ Ideal slow-cooker size: 3-qt.

1 gluten-free or regular roll-out pie crust (store-bought or homemade)

½ lb. bulk gluten-free chorizo sausage, browned, drained

¼ cup diced onion

¼ cup diced red pepper

1 cup shredded Mexican blend cheese

5 eggs

½ cup milk

¼ cup salsa

¼ tsp. chili powder

1. Line the crock with parchment paper so it comes up the sides. Hanging over the top is okay.

2. Lay the pie crust in the parchment-lined crock and press it into the shape of the crock. You'll want to make sure the crust goes up about 2½ inches on the sides. You can crimp the edges if you wish.

3. Sprinkle the chorizo, onion, red pepper, and Mexican blend cheese evenly around the crust.

4. In a bowl, whisk together the eggs, milk, salsa, and chili powder. Pour this mixture into the crock.

5. Lay paper towel over the top of the crock and secure it with the lid. Cook on Low for 3–4 hours.

6. When the quiche is cooked, gently lift the parchment paper out of the crock, then slice and serve.

NOTE
This recipe makes enough for seconds or leftovers!

Makes 4 servings. Using regular pie crust, each serving contains:

Calories: 640
Fat: 49g
Sodium: 1438mg
Carbs: 22g
Sugar: 3g
Protein: 28g

- Gluten-Free
- Nut-Free

Broccoli Cheddar Quiche

Hope Comerford, Clinton Township, MI

Prep. Time: 15 minutes 🌿 *Cooking Time: 3–4 hours* 🌿 *Ideal slow-cooker size: 3-qt.*

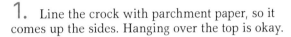

I gluten-free or regular roll-out pie crust (store-bought or homemade)

½ cup chopped broccoli florets

¼ cup diced onion

I cup shredded sharp cheddar cheese

5 eggs

¾ cups unsweetened almond milk

I tsp. garlic powder

I tsp. onion powder

½ tsp. no-salt seasoning blend

⅛ tsp. pepper

1. Line the crock with parchment paper, so it comes up the sides. Hanging over the top is okay.

2. Lay the pie crust in the parchment-lined crock and press it into the shape of the crock. You'll want to make sure the crust goes up about 2½ inches on the sides. You can crimp the edges if you wish.

3. Sprinkle the broccoli, onion, and cheddar evenly around the crust.

4. In a bowl, whisk together the eggs, almond milk, garlic powder, onion powder, no-salt seasoning blend, and pepper. Pour this mixture into the crock.

5. Lay paper towel over the top of the crock and secure it with the lid. Cook on Low for 3–4 hours.

6. When the quiche is cooked, gently lift the parchment paper out of the crock, then slice and serve.

NOTE
This recipe makes enough for seconds or leftovers!

Makes 4 servings. Using regular pie crust, each serving contains:

Calories: 390
Fat: 26g
Sodium: 399mg
Carbs: 21 g
Sugar: 1g
Protein: 14g

- Gluten-Free
- Soy-Free
- Vegetarian

Oatmeal

Janie Steele, Moore, OK

Prep. Time: 15 minutes ⚬ Cooking Time: 6–8 hours ⚬ Ideal slow-cooker size: 2-qt.

2 cups milk

¼ cup brown sugar

1 tablespoon butter

1 cup dry gluten-free or regular oats

1 cup fruit (chopped apples, blueberries, cranberries)

¼ teaspoon salt

½ teaspoon cinnamon

½ cup fat-free half-and-half

honey, *optional* (can be used for additional sweetness)

1. Spray inside of slow cooker with nonstick spray.

2. Combine all ingredients in a bowl except the half-and-half and honey, and mix.

3. Cover and cook 6–8 hours on Low.

4. Pour half-and-half in just before serving.

5. Add honey, if desired, to taste.

Makes 2 servings. Using ½ apples and ½ blueberries, each serving contains:

Calories: 560

Fat: 17g

Sodium: 523mg

Carbs: 85g

Sugar: 55g

Protein: 15g

- Gluten-Free
- Soy-Free
- Nut-Free
- Vegetarian

Oatmeal Cookie Oats

Hope Comerford, Clinton Township, MI

Prep. Time: 5 minutes ⚜ Cooking Time: 7 hours ⚜ Ideal slow-cooker size: 1½-qt.

1 cup gluten-free or regular steel cut oats

¼ cup raisins

¼ cup turbinado sugar

¼ tsp. vanilla extract

¼ tsp. cinnamon

⅛ tsp. salt

4 cups vanilla almond milk

1. Spray crock with nonstick spray.

2. Combine all ingredients in crock.

3. Cover and cook on Low for 7 hours.

NOTE
This recipe makes enough for seconds or leftovers!

Makes 4 servings. Each serving contains:

Calories: 233

Fat: 7g

Sodium: 272mg

Carbs: 40g

Sugar: 34g

Protein: 6g

- Gluten-Free
- Dairy-Free
- Soy-Free
- Vegetarian
- Vegan

Coco Loco Oatmeal

Hope Comerford, Clinton Township, MI

Prep. Time: 5 minutes ⚶ *Cooking Time: 7 hours* ⚶ *Ideal slow-cooker size: 1½-qt.*

I cup gluten-free steel cut oats

¼ cup gluten-free or regular sweetened shredded coconut

2 Tbsp. coconut sugar

¼ tsp. vanilla extract

⅛ tsp. salt

4 cups coconut milk

1. Spray crock with nonstick spray.

2. Combine all ingredients in crock.

3. Cover and cook on Low for 7 hours.

NOTE
This recipe makes enough for seconds or leftovers!

Makes 4 servings. When made with full-fat coconut milk, each serving contains:

Calories: 663
Fat: 64g
Sodium: 185mg
Carbs: 28g
Sugar: 22g
Protein: 9g

- Gluten-Free
- Dairy-Free
- Soy-Free
- Nut-Free
- Vegetarian
- Vegan

Cranberry Walnut Baked Oatmeal

Hope Comerford, Clinton Township, MI

Prep. Time: 10 minutes ⚶ Cooking Time: 2½–3 hours ⚶ Ideal slow-cooker size: 1½-qt.

1½ cups gluten-free or regular old-fashioned oats

¼ cup turbinado sugar

¼ cup dried cranberries

¼ cup chopped walnuts

¾ tsp. baking powder

¼ tsp. salt

1 egg

3 oz. unsweetened almond milk

1. Spray the crock with nonstick spray.

2. In a bowl, mix together the old-fashioned oats, sugar, cranberries, walnuts, baking powder, and salt.

3. Add the egg and milk to the oatmeal mixture and combine well. Pour this into the crock.

4. Cover and cook on Low for 2½–3 hours.

NOTE
This recipe makes enough for seconds or leftovers!

Makes 4 servings. Each serving contains:

Calories: 248
Fat: 15g
Sodium: 348mg
Carbs: 30g
Sugar: 28g
Protein: 10g

· Gluten-Free
· Dairy-Free
· Soy-Free
· Vegetarian

Blueberry Vanilla Oatmeal Bake

Hope Comerford, Clinton Township, MI

Prep. Time: 10 minutes ⚜ *Cooking Time: 2–3 hours* ⚜ *Ideal slow-cooker size: 2-qt.*

1½ cups gluten-free or regular old-fashioned oats

½ cup turbinado sugar

1 tsp. baking powder

½ tsp. vanilla extract

½ tsp. salt

½ cup unsweetened vanilla almond milk

1 egg

¼ cup coconut oil, melted

½ cup blueberries

1. Spray the crock with nonstick spray.

2. In a bowl, combine the old-fashioned oats, sugar, baking powder, vanilla, salt, unsweetened vanilla almond milk, egg, and coconut oil. Gently fold in the blueberries. Pour this mixture into the crock.

3. Cover and cook on Low for 2–3 hours.

NOTE
This recipe makes enough for seconds or leftovers!

Makes 4 servings. Each serving contains:

Calories: 281
Fat: 19g
Sodium: 475mg
Carbs: 23g
Sugar: 24g
Protein: 6g

- Gluten-Free
- Dairy-Free
- Soy-Free
- Nut-Free
- Vegetarian

Lemon Almond Blueberry Breakfast "Cakes"

Hope Comerford, Clinton Township, MI

Prep. Time: 25 minutes ⚶ Cooking Time: 3½–4 hours ⚶ Ideal slow-cooker size: 3-qt. oval

2 Tbsp. liquid egg whites

¼ cup coconut sugar

1 Tbsp. unsweetened applesauce

⅓ cup fresh lemon juice

½ tsp. lemon zest

2 cups almond flour

¾ tsp. baking powder

¼ tsp. baking soda

¼ tsp. salt

½ cup blueberries

1. Spray 3–4 small ramekins or individual baking dishes (about 1 each) with nonstick spray.

2. Mix together the egg whites, coconut sugar, applesauce, lemon juice, and lemon zest in a large bowl.

3. In a separate bowl, mix together the almond flour, baking powder, baking soda, and salt.

4. Slowly mix the dry ingredients into the wet ingredients. Stir only until just combined, then carefully fold in the blueberries. Pour the batter evenly into the ramekins or baking dishes.

5. Place a trivet, rack, mason jar lids, or crumpled-up foil in the bottom of the crock, then arrange the ramekins or baking dishes on top in the crock.

6. Place paper towel on top of the opening of the slow cooker. Secure it with the lid, then cook on Low for 3½–4 hours.

7. Eat with a spoon right out of the dish.

NOTE
This recipe makes enough for seconds or leftovers!

Makes 4 servings. Each serving contains:

Calories: 384
Fat: 28g
Sodium: 432mg
Carbs: 29g
Sugar: 11g
Protein: 23g

· Gluten-Free
· Soy-Free
· Vegetarian

Baked Apple Delight

Hope Comerford, Clinton Township, MI

Prep. Time: 25 minutes ⚬ *Cooking Time: 4 hours* ⚬ *Ideal slow-cooker size: 1½–2-qt.*

2 large apples (of your choice)

1 Tbsp. coconut sugar or brown sugar

¼ tsp. cinnamon

⅛ tsp. nutmeg

1 Tbsp. finely chopped pecans

⅓ cup blueberries

1½ Tbsp. melted coconut oil

Topping:

2 Tbsp. gluten-free or regular oats

½ tsp. coconut sugar

½ tsp. melted coconut oil

¼ tsp. cinnamon

1. Spray crock with nonstick spray.

2. Wash the apples. Cut the tops off, just enough to make them level and so the stems are removed. Scrape out the middle of the apples so that the cores are gone and some of the apple around it too. Leave at least ½ inch of apple around the sides. Be careful not to go through the bottom of the apple.

3. In a bowl, gently mix together the coconut sugar, cinnamon, nutmeg, pecans, blueberries, and coconut oil. Spoon this mixture evenly into the apples.

4. In a small bowl, mix the topping ingredients. Sprinkle this over the top of apples.

5. Place the apples in the crock. Cover and cook on Low for 4 hours.

Makes 2 servings. Each serving contains:

Calories: 320
Fat: 14g
Sodium: 17mg
Carbs: 49g
Sugar: 34g
Protein: 3 g

- Gluten-Free
- Dairy-Free
- Soy-Free
- Vegetarian
- Vegan

Cran-Apple Waffle Topping

Hope Comerford, Clinton Township, MI

Prep. Time: 10 minutes ⚬ Cooking Time: 3 hours ⚬ Ideal slow-cooker size: 1½-qt.

½ cup cranberries

1 cup peeled and diced apples

¼ cup freshly squeezed orange juice

1 tsp. orange zest

1½ Tbsp. coconut sugar or brown sugar

¼ tsp. cinnamon

1. Spray crock with nonstick spray.

2. Place all the listed ingredients in the crock.

3. Cover and cook on Low for 3 hours.

4. Use an immersion blender to make the contents of the crock smooth. You can use a blender, but be mindful that the contents will be very hot, so take precautions.

Makes 2 servings. Each serving contains:

Calories: 92

Fat: 0g

Sodium: 23mg

Carbs: 24g

Sugar: 18g

Protein: 0g

- Gluten-Free
- Dairy-Free
- Soy-Free
- Nut-Free
- Vegetarian
- Vegan

Appetizers & Snacks

Barbecue Chicken Lettuce Wraps

Hope Comerford, Clinton Township, MI

Prep. Time: 15 minutes ⚶ *Cooking Time: 2 hours* ⚶ *Ideal slow-cooker size: 1½-qt.*

⅓ lb. ground chicken, browned

¼ cup minced red onion

1 large clove garlic, minced

¼ of a 14½-oz. can diced tomatoes

½ cup sweet barbecue sauce (gluten-free or regular)

¼ tsp. salt

⅛ tsp. pepper

4–6 large lettuce leaves, washed and dried (romaine or iceberg work well)

1. Place all ingredients into crock except lettuce, and stir.

2. Cover and cook on Low for 2 hours.

3. To serve, spoon a little mixture in each piece of lettuce and wrap them up.

Per wrap, when making 6:

Calories: 105
Fat: 2g
Sodium: 352mg
Carbs: 16g
Sugar: 12g
Protein: 5g

- Gluten-Free
- Dairy-Free
- Nut-Free

Jalapeño Popper Chicken Taquitos

Hope Comerford, Clinton Township, MI

Prep. Time: 20 minutes ⚶ *Cooking Time: 5–6 hours* ⚶ *Baking Time: 10–15 minutes* ⚶ *Ideal slow-cooker size: 1½-qt.*

1½ boneless, skinless chicken breasts

3 Tbsp. gluten-free or regular chicken stock or water

4 oz. reduced-fat cream cheese

¼ cup chopped onion

2 Tbsp. chopped jarred jalapeño slices

1 clove garlic, minced

¼ tsp. chili powder

¼ tsp. cumin

4 gluten-free or regular tortilla wraps

¼ cup crumbled goat cheese

1. Place chicken, chicken stock or water, cream cheese, onion, jalapeños, garlic, chili powder, and cumin in crock.

2. Cover and cook on Low for 5–6 hours.

3. Remove chicken and shred it between 2 forks. Stir it back through the contents of the crock.

4. Preheat the oven to 425°F.

5. Line a baking sheet with parchment paper.

6. Lay out the 4 tortilla wraps. Spoon the chicken evenly among the 4 wraps, then sprinkle the goat cheese evenly among the 4 wraps as well.

7. Roll the wraps up tightly in a skinny log shape. Lay them on the parchment paper and spray them heavily with nonstick spray, or brush with a bit of olive oil.

8. Bake them for 10–15 minutes, or until the taquitos start to brown slightly.

Each taquito contains:

Calories: 305
Fat: 14g
Sodium: 638mg
Carbs: 18g
Sugar: 3g
Protein: 44g

- Gluten-Free
- Nut-Free

Mini-Magic Meat Balls

Carol Eveleth, Cheyenne, WY

Prep. Time: 15 minutes ⚶ *Cooking Time: 4–6 hours* ⚶ *Ideal slow-cooker size: 3-qt.*

I lb. ground beef
I cup bread crumbs
I egg, slightly beaten
I Tbsp. dried parsley flakes
I pkg. dry onion soup mix
I cup ketchup
⅓ cup lemon juice
⅓ cup grape jelly

1. Mix ground beef, bread crumbs, egg, parsley, and soup mix.

2. Shape into 1-inch balls.

3. Place in crock.

4. Mix together ketchup, lemon juice, and grape jelly. Pour this over the meatballs.

5. Cover and cook for 4–6 hours on Low.

NOTE
This recipe makes enough for seconds or leftovers!

Makes 4 servings. Each serving contains:

Calories: 471
Fat: 16g
Sodium: 1022mg
Carbs: 56g
Sugar: 41g
Protein: 27g

• Dairy-free
• Nut-Free

Drunken Sausage Bites

Hope Comerford, Clinton Township, MI

Prep. Time: 5 minutes ♣ *Cooking Time: 2 hours* ♣ *Ideal slow-cooker size: 1½-qt.*

3 sweet Italian sausage links, cut into ½-inch pieces (gluten-free or regular)

½ cup merlot

1 Tbsp. red currant jelly

½ tsp. Worcestershire sauce (gluten-free or regular)

1. Spray crock with nonstick spray.

2. Place the Italian sausage in the crock.

3. In a bowl, combine the merlot, red currant jelly, and Worcestershire sauce. Pour this over the sausages and stir them to coat all evenly.

4. Cover and cook on Low for 2 hours.

NOTE
This recipe makes enough for seconds or leftovers!

Makes 4 servings. Each serving contains:

Calories: 242
Fat: 16g
Sodium: 1160mg
Carbs: 7g
Sugar: 5g
Protein: 11g

- Gluten-Free
- Dairy-Free
- Nut-Free

Sausage Sweeties

Hope Comerford, Clinton Township, MI

Prep. Time: 20 minutes ⚬ Cooking Time: 4–5 hours ⚬ Ideal slow-cooker size: 2-qt.

3 chicken sausage links, cut into ½-inch diagonal pieces (gluten-free or regular)

¼ cup chopped red pepper

3 Tbsp. chopped onion

1 clove garlic, minced

3 Tbsp. chili sauce

3 Tbsp. apple jelly

½ tsp. gluten-free or regular soy sauce

¼ tsp. salt

¼ tsp. ginger

⅛ tsp. pepper

½ tsp. cornstarch

½ tsp. water

1. Place chicken sausage, red pepper, and onion in crock.

2. In a small bowl, mix together the garlic, chili sauce, apple jelly, soy sauce, salt, ginger, and pepper. Pour this over the contents of the crock.

3. Cover and cook on Low for 3¾–4¾ hours.

4. Mix together the cornstarch and water, then stir it through the contents of the crock. Cook on High for an additional 15 minutes.

NOTE
This recipe makes enough for seconds or leftovers!

Makes 4 servings. Each serving contains:

Calories: 98
Fat: 2g
Sodium: 514mg
Carbs: 15g
Sugar: 13g
Protein: 4g

- Gluten-Free
- Dairy-Free
- Nut-Free

Buffalo Chicken Dip (Hot and Spicy)

Ne'cole Cichowlas, Chesterfield, MI

Prep. Time: 5 minutes ⚶ *Cooking Time: 4 hours* ⚶ *Ideal slow-cooker size: 1½-qt.*

2 oz. canned chicken (about ½ can), shredded well

¼ cup ranch dressing

¼ cup Frank's RedHot Original Cayenne Pepper Sauce

2 tablespoons Frank's RedHot Buffalo Wings Sauce

2 oz. cream cheese

½ cup shredded cheddar cheese

celery sticks or tortilla chips for dipping

1. Place all ingredients in crock.

2. Cover and cook on High for 1 hour and then mix well.

3. Continue to cook on Low 2–3 hours.

4. Stir before serving.

Serving Suggestion:

We love to eat this dip with tortilla chips, but experiment with your favorite snack. This dip saves well and I enjoy eating it cold the next day!

NOTE
This recipe makes enough for seconds or leftovers!

Makes 4 servings. Each serving contains:

Calories: 198
Fat: 13g
Sodium: 1030mg
Carbs: 2g
Sugar: 1g
Protein: 8g

- Nut-Free
- Gluten-Free

Spicy Sausage Cheese Dip

Laura Elwood, Milford, MI

Prep. Time: 15 minutes ⚶ *Cooking Time: 30 minutes* ⚶ *Ideal slow-cooker size: 2-qt.*

8 oz. spicy bulk sausage

5 oz. diced tomatoes and green chilies

4 oz. (½ pkg.) cream cheese

1. Brown the sausage in a pan.

2. Add the cooked sausage, tomatoes, and cream cheese to the slow cooker.

3. Cover and cook on Low, stirring every so often until the cheese is melted.

4. Once hot and everything is combined, serve with tortilla chips and raw veggies like cauliflower, broccoli, or zucchini.

Favorite memory of sharing this recipe:

The first time I had this dip, I was standing in a new friend's kitchen. We stayed up super late chatting about life and business. She gave me amazing business advice and made me feel so welcome on this new adventure I was on.

NOTE

This recipe makes enough for seconds or leftovers!

Makes 4 servings. Each serving contains:

Calories: 265
Fat: 23g
Sodium: 566mg
Carbs: 4g
Sugar: 3g
Protein: 11g

• Nut-Free

Chip Dip

Janeen Troyer, Fairview, MI

Prep. Time: 20 minutes ⚶ Cooking Time: 1½–2 hours ⚶ Ideal slow-cooker size: 1½-qt.

¼ lb. bulk sausage, browned

8 oz. Velveeta cheese, cut into chunks

¼ cup salsa

2 tablespoons milk

hot sauce, *optional*

1. Place the sausage and Velveeta into the crock.

2. Add the salsa and milk. You may need to add more milk if it is too thick. You can also add hot sauce to make it spicier.

3. Cover and cook on Low for 1½–2 hours. Stir frequently.

Serving Suggestion:

Serve with tortilla chips.

NOTE
This recipe makes enough for seconds or leftovers!

Makes 4 servings. Each serving contains:

Calories: 240

Fat: 16g

Sodium: 1101mg

Carbs: 7.5g

Sugar: 5g

Protein: 8.5g

• Nut-Free

Cheesy Burger Dip

Carol Eveleth, Cheyenne, WY

Prep. Time: 5 minutes ⚜ *Cooking Time: 1½–3 hours* ⚜ *Ideal slow-cooker size: 1½-qt.*

¼ lb. ground beef, browned
¼ lb. Velveeta cheese, cubed
2 oz. mild taco sauce
¼ tsp. chili powder
¼ tsp. Worcestershire sauce
⅛ tsp. garlic salt

1. Place all ingredients in crock.

2. Cover and cook on Low for 1½–3 hours.

3. Stir once when cheese is melted. Eat with your favorite chips.

Favorite memory of sharing this recipe:

If memory serves me correctly, my husband and I had this dip, chips, and a special drink on New Year's Eve while waiting for the year 2000 to come!

NOTE
This recipe makes enough for seconds or leftovers!

Makes 4 servings. Each serving contains:

Calories: 197
Fat: 11g
Sodium: 677mg
Carbs: 9g
Sugar: 5g
Protein: 12g

• Nut-Free
• Gluten-Free

Mexi Dip

Hope Comerford, Clinton Township, MI

Prep. Time: 10 minutes ☙ *Cooking Time: 2 hours* ☙ *Ideal slow-cooker size: 1½-qt.*

4 oz. reduced-fat cream cheese

¼ cup nonfat plain Greek yogurt

½ cup shredded Parmesan cheese

½ cup salsa

1 tsp. gluten-free or regular taco seasoning

tortilla chips

1. Combine cream cheese, Greek yogurt, Parmesan cheese, salsa, and taco seasoning in crock.

2. Cover and cook on Low for 2 hours.

3. Serve with tortilla chips.

NOTE
This recipe makes enough for seconds or leftovers!

Makes 4 servings. Each serving contains:

Calories: 127
Fat: 9g
Sodium: 777mg
Carbs: 5g
Sugar: 1.5 g
Protein: 10g

- Gluten-Free
- Soy-Free
- Nut-Free
- Vegetarian

Jalapeño Dip

Hope Comerford, Clinton Township, MI

Prep. Time: 10 minutes ⚹ *Cooking Time: 2–3 hours* ⚹ *Ideal slow-cooker size: 1½-qt.*

½ cup vegetarian gluten-free or regular refried beans

½ cup salsa

2 Tbsp. reduced-fat cream cheese, softened

¼ cup chopped onion

¼ cup diced jarred jalapeños (hot or mild)

¼ tsp. chili powder

¼ tsp. garlic powder

¼ tsp. salt

gluten-free or regular tortilla chips

1. Combine the refried beans, salsa, reduced-fat cream cheese, onion, jalapeños, chili powder, garlic powder, and salt in the crock.

2. Cover and cook on Low for 2–3 hours.

3. Serve with tortilla chips for dipping.

NOTE
This recipe makes enough for seconds or leftovers!

Makes 4 servings. Not including tortilla chips, each serving contains:

Calories: 35
Fat: < 1g
Sodium: 613mg
Carbs: 8g
Sugar: 1.5g
Protein: 2g

- Gluten-Free
- Soy-Free
- Nut-Free
- Vegetarian

Crab Dip

Hope Comerford, Clinton Township, MI

Prep. Time: 5 minutes ☆ Cooking Time: 2 hours ☆ Ideal slow-cooker size: 1½-qt.

¼ cup nonfat plain Greek yogurt

4 oz. reduced-fat cream cheese, softened

2 Tbsp. fresh minced onion

1 clove garlic, minced

½ lb. gluten-free or regular imitation or lump crabmeat

gluten-free or regular crackers

1. Combine the Greek yogurt, cream cheese, minced onion, garlic, and crabmeat in the crock.

2. Cover and cook on Low for 2 hours.

3. Serve with crackers for dipping.

NOTE
This recipe makes enough for seconds or leftovers!

Makes 4 servings. Not including crackers, each serving contains:

Calories: 135
Fat: 6g
Sodium: 430mg
Carbs: 6g
Sugar: 0.5g
Protein: 11g

- Gluten-Free
- Soy-Free
- Nut-Free

Swiss Cheese Dip

Ne'cole Cichowlas, Chesterfield, MI

Prep. Time: 5 minutes ⚮ *Cooking Time: 3–4 hours* ⚮ *Ideal slow-cooker size: 1½-qt.*

8 oz. finely shredded Swiss cheese

½ cup mayonnaise

½ medium sweet onion, finely chopped (almost shaved)

Triscuits or your favorite cracker, for serving

1. Place cheese, mayonnaise, and onion in slow cooker.

2. Cover and cook on Low for 3–4 hours.

3. Stir well and serve with Triscuits or your favorite crackers.

NOTE
This recipe makes enough for seconds or leftovers!

Makes 4 servings. Without crackers, each serving contains:

Calories: 403
Fat: 23g
Sodium: 289mg
Carbs: 5g
Sugar: 1g
Protein: 15.5g

• Nut-Free
• Vegetarian

Bacony Spinach & Artichoke Dip

Hope Comerford, Clinton Township, MI

Prep. Time: 10 minutes ⚶ Cooking Time: 3 hours ⚶ Ideal slow-cooker size: 2-qt.

1 slice bacon, cooked, chopped

7 oz. jarred or canned artichoke hearts, drained, coarsely chopped

3 oz. fresh spinach, chopped

2 cloves garlic, minced

3 Tbsp. minced shallot

¼ cup mayonnaise

2 oz. reduced-fat cream cheese, softened

¼ cup shredded mozzarella cheese

½ tsp. salt

⅛ tsp. pepper

gluten-free or regular crackers, for dipping

1. Spray crock with nonstick spray.

2. In a bowl, mix together all of the ingredients, then place them into the crock.

3. Cover and cook on Low for 3 hours.

4. Serve with crackers for dipping.

NOTE
This recipe makes enough for seconds or leftovers!

Makes 4 servings. Using canned artichokes, without crackers, each serving contains:

Calories: 178
Fat: 14.5g
Sodium: 655mg
Carbs: 5.5g
Sugar: 0g
Protein: 4.5g

- Gluten-Free
- Nut-Free

Italian Veggie Spread

Hope Comerford, Clinton Township, MI

Prep. Time: 20 minutes ⚜ *Cooking Time: 5 hours* ⚜ *Ideal slow-cooker size: 2-qt.*

¼ lb. Roma tomatoes, cut into ½-inch pieces

3 oz. eggplant, peeled, cut into ½-inch pieces

3 oz. zucchini, cut into ½-inch pieces

1 stalk celery, diced

¼ cup chopped sweet onion

2 Tbsp. freshly chopped parsley

3 Tbsp. pitted Kalamata olives, roughly chopped

1 tsp. capers

2 tsp. tomato paste

2 tsp. balsamic vinegar

¼ tsp. salt

⅛ tsp. pepper

gluten-free crackers or pita crisps, or regular crackers or pita crisps

1. Spray crock with nonstick spray.

2. Place Roma tomatoes, eggplant, zucchini, celery, onion, parsley, Kalamata olives, capers, tomato paste, balsamic vinegar, salt, and pepper into crock.

3. Cover and cook on Low for 5 hours.

4. Serve hot, cold, or room temperature with the crackers or pita crisps.

NOTE
This recipe makes enough for seconds or leftovers!

Makes 4 servings. Without crackers, each serving contains:

Calories: 34	• Gluten-Free
Fat: 2g	• Dairy-Free
Sodium: 324mg	• Soy-Free
Carbs: 6g	• Nut-Free
Sugar: 3g	• Vegetarian
Protein: 1g	• Vegan

Ranch Snack Mix

Hope Comerford, Clinton Township, MI

Prep. Time: 15 minutes ⚶ *Cooking Time: 2–2½ hours* ⚶ *Cooling Time: 30 minutes* ⚶ *Ideal slow-cooker size: 2-qt.*

1 cup Cheerios

½ cup gluten-free or regular rice square cereal

¼ cup unsalted cashews

2 Tbsp. sunflower seeds

¼ of a 1 oz. gluten-free or regular dry ranch salad dressing mix packet

½ Tbsp. olive oil

1. Spray crock with nonstick spray.

2. Place Cheerios, rice square cereal, cashews, and sunflower seeds into crock.

3. Sprinkle the dry ranch salad dressing mix all over the contents of the crock and drizzle with the olive oil. Toss gently.

4. Cover and cook on Low for 2–2½ hours, stirring every 30 minutes.

5. Spread mixture out onto a parchment lined baking sheet to cool for about 30 minutes. Store in an airtight container for up to 2 weeks.

NOTE
This recipe makes enough for seconds or leftovers!

Makes 4 servings. Each serving contains:

Calories: 128
Fat: 8g
Sodium: 201mg
Carbs: 17.5g
Sugar: 1g
Protein: 3g

• Gluten-Free
• Vegetarian

Candied & Spiced Pecans

Hope Comerford, Clinton Township, MI

Prep. Time: 10 minutes ⚜ *Cooking Time: 3 hours* ⚜ *Cooling Time: 1 hour* ⚜ *Ideal slow-cooker size: 2-qt.*

1 ½ cups pecans

½ egg white

½ tsp. vanilla extract

3 Tbsp. brown sugar

½ cup coconut sugar

½ tsp. cinnamon

¼ tsp. chili powder

3 tsp. water

1. Spray crock with nonstick spray.

2. Place the pecans in the crock.

3. In a small bowl, whisk together the ½ egg white and vanilla until it is frothy. Pour this over the pecans and stir until they're evenly coated.

4. In a separate bowl, mix the brown sugar, coconut sugar, cinnamon, and chili powder. Pour this over the nuts and stir until they're evenly coated.

5. Cover and cook on Low for 3 hours, stirring every 20 minutes. When there are 20 minutes left of cooking, stir in the water and recover the crock.

6. When cooking time is over, spread the pecans out on a parchment paper–lined baking sheet. Let cool for 1 hour. Store in an airtight container for up to 2 weeks.

NOTE

Save leftovers in a mason jar or a sealed plastic bag! Toss a handful on a salad or on your yogurt.

Makes 6 servings. Each serving contains:

Calories: 280
Fat: 20g
Sodium: 49g
Carbs: 25g
Sugar: 17.5g
Protein: 3.5g

- Gluten-Free
- Soy-Free
- Vegetarian

Soups, Stews & Chilis

Minestrone Soup

Maria Shevlin, Sicklerville, NJ

Prep. Time: 30 minutes ⚶ Cooking Time: 8 hours ⚶ Ideal slow-cooker size: 3-qt.

½ cup diced smoked ham

½ medium onion, finely chopped

2 cloves garlic, minced

I medium carrot, diced

2 ribs celery, diced

I zucchini, diced

I small russet potato, peeled and diced

½ cup shredded green cabbage

I small can picante tomato sauce

6–8 mushrooms, diced

2 cups vegetable broth

I Tbsp. dried parsley

½ Tbsp. dried sweet basil

salt, to taste

½ cup elbow macaroni, cooked al dente and drained, *optional*

1. Add everything but the macaroni into the crock and mix well.

2. Cover and cook on Low for 8 hours. Add the macaroni 15 minutes before serving, if desired.

3. Ladle into bowls and eat with a slice of hearty crusty Italian bread, if desired.

Variation:

If you want a different meat in this, you can brown ½ lb. of ground turkey, drain the juices, and add that to the slow cooker instead of the ham.

Makes 2 servings. With macaroni and no additional salt, each serving contains:

Calories: 314

Fat: 6.5g

Sodium: 668mg

Carbs: 31.5g

Sugar: 12g

Protein: 16.5g

- Nut-Free
- Dairy-Free
- Soy-Free

Simple Salsa Soup

Hope Comerford, Clinton Township, MI

Prep. Time: 10 minutes ⚶ *Cooking Time: 4–5 hours* ⚶ *Ideal slow-cooker size: 3-qt.*

½ lb. browned gluten-free or regular bulk Italian turkey sausage

I cup canned navy beans, drained and rinsed

1½ cups gluten-free or regular salsa

3 cups gluten-free or regular chicken stock

½ tsp. salt

I clove garlic, minced

1. Combine all the listed ingredients in the crock.

2. Cover and cook on Low for 4–5 hours.

NOTE
This recipe makes enough for seconds or leftovers!

Makes 4 servings. Each serving contains:

Calories: 178
Fat: 12.5g
Sodium: 1841mg
Carbs: 35g
Sugar: 7.5g
Protein: 28g

• Gluten-Free
• Dairy-Free
• Nut-Free

Cowboy-Mexi Soup

MarJanita Geigley, Lancaster, PA

Prep. Time: 15 minutes ❦ Cooking Time: 2–3 hours ❦ Ideal slow-cooker size: 3 qt.

½ lb. ground beef, browned, drained

½ onion, chopped

½ cup water

½ Tbsp. ground cumin

14-oz. can chicken broth

14½-oz. can of diced tomatoes

2 cups chopped cooked onion

5 oz. corn kernels

4 oz. diced green chili peppers

cheese, *optional*

tortilla strips, *optional*

1. Combine all ingredients except cheese and tortilla chips into crock and stir.

2. Cook on Low for 2–3 hours.

3. Serve topped with cheese and tortilla strips, if desired.

NOTE
This recipe makes enough for seconds or leftovers!

Makes 4 servings. Without cheese or tortilla strips, each serving contains:

Calories: 189
Fat: 6.5g
Sodium: 506mg
Carbs: 25g
Sugar: 9g
Protein: 14g

- Dairy-Free
- Soy-Free
- Nut-Free

Easy Soup

Janie Steele, Moore, OK

Prep. Time: 30 minutes ⚬ *Cooking Time: 5–6 hours* ⚬ *Ideal slow-cooker size: 3-qt.*

1 lb. ground beef, browned and drained (can use turkey, sausage, meatballs instead of beef)

4 cups beef broth

1 cup water

1 bay leaf

¼ cup diced carrots

¼ cup diced potatoes

¼ cup celery, sliced

¼ cup chopped onion

14½-oz. can diced tomatoes

salt and pepper, to taste

1. Add all ingredients to crock.

2. Cover and cook 5–6 hours on Low.

3. Remove bay leaf before serving.

NOTE

Vegetable amounts can vary due to preference.

This recipe makes enough for seconds or leftovers!

Makes 4 servings. With no additional salt, each serving contains:

Calories: 258
Fat: 13.5g
Sodium: 971mg
Carbs: 11g
Sugar: 4g
Protein: 21g

• Dairy-Free
• Nut-Free

Chicken Tortilla Soup

Maria Shevlin, Sicklerville, NJ

Prep. Time: 30 minutes ⚮ *Cooking Time: 6 hours* ⚮ *Ideal slow-cooker size: 3 qt.*

2 stalks of celery, sliced down the center lengthwise, then chopped

½ medium onion, chopped

½ cup frozen corn

½ can black beans, drained and rinsed

3 cups chicken stock

1 cup water

16 oz. picante sauce

4 cloves garlic, minced

½ tsp. cumin

1 tsp. chili powder

1 tsp. paprika

1 cup diced precooked chicken

Optional toppings:

green onion, chopped

tortilla strips

sour cream (or plain Greek yogurt)

Mexican blend or taco shredded cheese

jalapeños

1. Place the celery and onion in the crock.

2. Add the corn and black beans.

3. Mix well, then add the chicken stock, water, picante sauce, garlic, cumin, chili powder, and paprika.

4. Place the precooked chicken into the crock and mix well.

5. Cover and cook on Low for 6 hours.

6. Ladle into bowls and top with any or all of the optional toppings you want.

NOTE
This recipe makes enough for seconds or leftovers!

Makes 4 servings. Without toppings, each serving contains:

Calories: 163
Fat: 3g
Sodium: 831mg
Carbs: 20g
Sugar: 8.5g
Protein: 11g

• Nut-Free

Quilters Soup

Janie Steele, Moore, OK

Prep. Time: 30 minutes   Cooking Time: 3–4 hours   Ideal slow-cooker size: 3-qt.

¾ cup diced cooked chicken

14½-oz. can chicken broth

½ of a 24-oz. jar Prego Roasted Garlic & Herb Italian sauce

1 Tbsp. parsley

¼ tsp. thyme

1½ cups cooked brown rice

1. Combine all ingredients in crock.

2. Cover and cook 3–4 hours on Low.

NOTE
This recipe makes enough for seconds or leftovers!

Makes 4 servings. Each serving contains:

Calories: 190
Fat: 4g
Sodium: 613mg
Carbs: 27g
Sugar: 7.5g
Protein: 11g

- Dairy-Free
- Nut-Free

Beef and Quinoa Soup

Hope Comerford, Clinton Township, MI

Prep. Time: 15 minutes ⚜ *Cooking Time: 7–9 hours* ⚜ *Ideal slow-cooker size: 3-qt.*

¾ lb. chuck roast, cubed

I medium-sized carrot, chopped

I stalk celery, chopped

4 oz. baby bella mushrooms, diced

½ cup chopped yellow onion

I Tbsp. fresh minced onion

2 tsp. tomato paste

½ tsp. basil

½ tsp. thyme

½ tsp. salt

⅛ tsp. pepper

I bay leaf

4 cups gluten-free or regular low-sodium beef stock

I tsp. gluten-free or regular soy sauce

½ tsp. gluten-free or regular Worcestershire sauce

¼ cup quinoa

1. Place all ingredients into the crock and give it a couple stirs.

2. Cover and cook on Low for 7–9 hours.

3. Remove the bay leaf before serving.

NOTE
This recipe makes enough for seconds or leftovers!

Makes 4 servings. Each serving contains:

Calories: 292

Fat: 17g

Sodium: 545mg

Carbs: 12.5g

Sugar: 2.5g

Protein: 22g

- Gluten-Free
- Dairy-Free
- Nut-Free

Black Bean Taco Soup

Hope Comerford, Clinton Township, MI

Prep. Time: 10 minutes ⚬ Cooking Time: 5–6 hours ⚬ Ideal slow-cooker size: 3-qt.

14½-oz. can black beans, drained and rinsed

½ of 14½-oz. can diced tomatoes

¼ cup chopped onion

¼ cup diced green pepper

½ of a jalapeño pepper, seeded and diced

5 cups gluten-free or regular vegetable stock

1 Tbsp. gluten-free or regular taco seasoning

1. Combine all ingredients in the crock.

2. Cover and cook on Low for 5–6 hours.

NOTE
This recipe makes enough for seconds or leftovers!

Makes 4 servings. Prepared with vegetable broth, each serving contains:

Calories: 137
Fat: 1g
Sodium: 27mg
Carbs: 24g
Sugar: 3.5g
Protein: 7g

- Gluten-Free
- Dairy-Free
- Nut-Free
- Vegetarian
- Vegan

Cabbage Soup

Hope Comerford, Clinton Township, MI

Prep. Time: 10 minutes ✿ *Cooking Time: 4–5 hours* ✿ *Ideal slow-cooker size: 3-qt.*

1 cup thinly sliced cabbage

14½-oz. can diced tomatoes

½ cup chopped onion

¼ cup diced celery

¼ cup diced carrots

1 clove garlic, minced

½ tsp. salt

½ tsp. oregano

½ tsp. basil

⅛ tsp. pepper

5 cups tomato juice

1. Combine all ingredients in crock.

2. Cover and cook on Low for 4–5 hours.

NOTE
This recipe makes enough for seconds or leftovers!

Makes 4 servings. Each serving contains:

Calories: 111
Fat: 0g
Sodium: 1163mg
Carbs: 22.5g
Sugar: 14g
Protein: 4g

- Gluten-Free
- Dairy-Free
- Soy-Free
- Nut-Free
- Vegetarian
- Vegan

Beef Stew For Two

Michele Ruvola, Vestal, NY

Prep. Time: 15 minutes 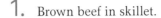 *Cooking Time: 8 hours*   *Ideal slow-cooker size: 3-qt.*

1 lb. cubed stew beef

10½-oz. can condensed golden
mushroom soup

½ cup chopped onion

1 Tbsp. Worcestershire sauce

¼ cup water

wide egg noodles

4 oz. cream cheese

1. Brown beef in skillet.

2. Spray crock with nonstick cooking spray.

3. Place beef, soup, onion, Worcestershire sauce, and water in crock.

4. Cover and cook on Low for 8 hours.

5. When ready to eat, cook about ½ the egg noodles according to package directions. Save remaining noodles to cook and eat with leftovers.

6. Stir cream cheese into stew just before serving.

7. Serve stew on top of noodles.

*Divided into 2 portions, not including egg noodles,
each portion contains:*

Calories: 752

Fat: 55g

Sodium: 1297mg

Carbs: 21g

Sugar: 6.5g

Protein: 56g

•   Nut-Free

Beef Stew

Carol Eveleth, Cheyenne, WY

Prep. Time: 20 minutes ⚜ *Cooking Time: 4–8 hours* ⚜ *Ideal slow-cooker size: 3-qt.*

1 lb. cubed stew beef
3 large carrots, chunked
1 small onion, chopped
2 stalks celery, chopped
3 medium potatoes, chunked
1 tsp. salt
¼ tsp. black pepper
3 Tbsp. instant tapioca
3 Tbsp. ketchup
¾ cup tomato juice
¾ cup water

1. Put raw beef, carrots, onion, celery, and potatoes in crock in layers.

2. Sprinkle seasonings and tapioca over this.

3. Add ketchup, tomato juice, and water.

4. Cover and cook for 4–6 hours on High or 6–8 hours on Low.

NOTE
This recipe makes enough for seconds or leftovers!

Makes 4 servings. Each serving contains:

Calories: 400
Fat: 15g
Sodium: 982mg
Carbs: 39g
Sugar: 7.5g
Protein: 28g

- Gluten-Free
- Dairy-Free
- Soy-Free
- Nut-Free

Winter Stew

Jane Geigley, Lancaster, PA

Prep. Time: 10 minutes ❧ *Cooking Time: 4–5 hours* ❧ *Ideal slow-cooker size: 3-qt.*

2 Tbsp. all-purpose flour

⅛ tsp. pepper

1 lb. beef, cut into 1-inch cubes

1 Tbsp. vegetable oil

1 medium onion, diced

2 stalks celery, diced

10½-oz. can condensed beef broth

½ cup water

½ tsp. crushed dried thyme leaves

1 bay leaf

4 medium carrots, cut into 1-inch pieces

3 medium potatoes, cut into quarters

1 tsp. seasoned pepper

1 Tbsp. chives

1. Mix flour and ⅛ tsp. pepper.

2. Coat beef with flour mixture.

3. In pan over medium heat, heat oil.

4. Add beef, onion, and celery and cook until browned on all sides. Place in crock.

5. Add broth, water, thyme, bay leaf, carrots, potatoes, seasoned pepper, and chives to crock.

6. Cover and cook on High for 4–5 hours.

Serving Suggestion:
Serve with toasted
French bread and butter.

NOTE
This recipe makes enough for seconds or leftovers!

Makes 4 servings. Each serving contains:

Calories: 415
Fat: 18.5g
Sodium: 605mg
Carbs: 34g
Sugar: 6g
Protein: 31g

· Dairy-Free
· Nut-Free

Quick Stew

Janie Steele, Moore, OK

Prep. Time: 30 minutes ⚬ *Cooking Time: 5–6 hours* ⚬ *Ideal slow-cooker size: 3-qt.*

2 cups water

2 potatoes, diced

2-oz. pkg. dry onion soup

16 oz. frozen vegetables

1 lb. browned beef or turkey, drained

4 slices bacon, browned and crumbled

salt and pepper, to taste

2 cloves garlic, chopped

1 Tbsp. sugar

1 Tbsp. flour

14½-oz. can diced tomatoes

1. Combine all ingredients in crock.

2. Cover and cook on Low for 5–6 hours.

NOTE

This recipe makes enough for seconds or leftovers!

Makes 4 servings. Each serving contains:

Calories: 355

Fat: 14g

Sodium: 872mg

Carbs: 27.5g

Sugar: 6.5g

Protein: 23.5g

• Nut-Free

Comforting Stew

Hope Comerford, Clinton Township, MI

Prep. Time: 20 minutes ⚘ *Cooking Time: 6–7 hours* ⚘ *Ideal slow-cooker size: 3-qt.*

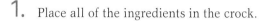

4 gluten-free or regular Italian sausage links, cut on an angle into ½-inch slices

¼ cup chopped onion

¼ cup chopped carrot

¼ cup chopped celery

½ cup diced peeled potatoes

I clove garlic, minced

¾ tsp. salt

½ tsp. basil

½ tsp. oregano

4 cups gluten-free or regular chicken stock

1. Place all of the ingredients in the crock.

2. Cover and cook on Low for 6–7 hours.

NOTE
This recipe makes enough for seconds or leftovers!

Makes 4 servings. Each serving contains:

Calories: 290
Fat: 22g
Sodium: 1813mg
Carbs: 12g
Sugar: 4.5g
Protein: 15.5g

- Gluten-Free
- Dairy-Free
- Nut-Free

Asian Short Rib "Stoup"

Dena Mell-Dorchy, Royal Oak, MI

Prep. Time: 30 minutes & Cooking Time: 7½ hours & Ideal slow-cooker size: 3-qt.

2 lbs. boneless short ribs

3 Tbsp. shredded ginger

1 tsp. minced garlic

¼ cup low-sodium soy sauce

1 Tbsp. toasted sesame oil

1 tsp. cumin

½ tsp. black pepper

2 carrots, cut into small pieces

1 sweet onion, cut into small wedges

1 cup beef broth

3 Tbsp. brown sugar

½ lb. baby bok choy, coarsely chopped

½ Tbsp. rice wine vinegar

2 green onions, chopped

steamed rice or rice noodles, for serving, *optional*

1. Spray slower cooker with nonstick spray.

2. Combine the short ribs, ginger, garlic, soy sauce, sesame oil, cumin, and pepper in the slow cooker and mix to combine.

3. Add carrots, onion, beef broth, and brown sugar. Mix.

4. Cover and cook on Low for 6–7 hours.

5. Add bok choy, vinegar, and green onions and cook until the bok choy is soft.

6. Serve on its own or with rice or noodles.

Favorite memory of sharing this recipe:
This was the first successful slow cooker meal I made for my husband after we were married. It is still his favorite.

NOTE
This recipe makes enough for seconds or leftovers!

Makes 4 servings. Without rice or noodles, each serving contains:

Calories: 518
Fat: 27g
Sodium: 951mg
Carbs: 15g
Sugar: 11g
Protein: 45.5g

• Dairy-Free
• Nut-Free

Chunky Chili

Jennifer Freed, Rockingham, VA

Prep. Time: 20 minutes ⚶ *Cooking Time: 5–6 hours* ⚶ *Ideal slow-cooker size: 3-qt.*

½ lb. 90% lean ground beef

1 small onion, chopped

½ Tbsp. chili powder

¾ tsp. ground cumin

16-oz. can diced tomatoes, undrained

½ of a 15-oz. can pinto beans, drained and rinsed

¼ cup prepared salsa

salt and pepper, to taste

¼ cup shredded cheddar cheese

⅛ cup diced onions

2 tsp. sliced black olives

1. Heat large skillet over medium heat.

2. Add beef and onion; cook until beef is browned and onion is tender.

3. Drain fat.

4. Place beef mixture, chili powder, cumin, tomatoes, beans, and salsa in slow cooker; stir.

5. Cover; cook on Low 5–6 hours or until flavors are blended and chili is bubbly.

6. Season with salt and pepper, to taste.

7. Serve with cheese, onions, and olives.

Serving suggestion:
Serve this recipe with tossed green salad and corn muffins.

Makes 2 servings. With toppings included and no additional salt, each serving contains:

Calories: 400	
Fat: 17g	• Nut-Free
Sodium: 716mg	
Carbs: 37.5g	
Sugar: 9.5g	
Protein: 27g	

Easy Chili

Janie Steele, Moore, OK

Prep. Time: 20 min. ⚥ *Cooking Time: 2–4 hours* ⚥ *Ideal slow-cooker size: 3-qt.*

19-oz. can minestrone soup

15-oz. can ranch-style beans

10-oz. can Ro-Tel tomatoes with green chilies

½ lb. browned ground beef

1. Mix all ingredients together in crock.

2. Cover and cook on Low 3–4 hours or High for 2–3 hours.

NOTE
This recipe makes enough for seconds or leftovers!

Makes 4 servings. Each serving contains:

Calories: 280
Fat: 10g
Sodium: 1218mg
Carbs: 29.5g
Sugar: 6g
Protein: 17.5g

• Nut-Free

No Fuss Chili

Michele Ruvola, Vestal, NY

Prep. Time: 15 minutes ❧ Cooking Time: 6–8 hours ❧ Ideal slow-cooker size: 3-qt.

1 lb. ground beef
½ cup chopped onion
1 tsp. salt
½ tsp. pepper
15-oz. can tomato sauce
1½ tsp. cumin
⅛ tsp. garlic powder
1½ tsp. paprika
2½ tsp. chili powder
14½-oz. can red kidney beans
water or beef broth to thin sauce,
optional

Optional serving ingredients:
Shredded cheese, scallions, sour cream,
jalapeños, baked potatoes

1. Sauté ground beef in skillet until almost brown.

2. Add onion with salt and pepper. Finish browning meat.

3. Transfer to slow cooker.

4. Add tomato sauce, spices, and beans.

5. Add water or beef broth to thin sauce to desired consistency.

6. Cover and cook on Low 6–8 hours.

7. Serve in bowl or on top of baked potato with toppings of your choice.

Favorite memory of sharing this recipe:

When we go Christmas tree shopping we put this in the slow cooker and come home to wonderful smells in the house. As we decorate the tree we eat a warm, filling bowl of chili on baked potatoes.

NOTE
This recipe makes enough for seconds or leftovers!

Makes 4 servings. Without optional toppings, each serving contains:

Calories: 340
Fat: 12.5g
Sodium: 1436mg
Carbs: 29g
Sugar: 6g
Protein: 27g

• Gluten-Free
• Nut-Free

Easy Weeknight Chili

Carrie Fritz, Meridian, ID

Prep. Time: 15 ❧ Cooking Time: 4–6 hours ❧ Ideal slow-cooker size: 3-qt.

½ lb. ground beef, browned

14½-oz. can petite diced tomatoes

8-oz. can tomato sauce

15½-oz. can of seasoned chili beans

15½-oz. can of beans (northern, black or kidney beans are good)

½ of a chili seasoning packet

½ green pepper, diced, *optional*

½ onion, diced, *optional*

1. Add all the ingredients in the slow cooker. Cover and cook on Low for 4–6 hours.

2. Good toppings include grated cheese, sour cream, or crushed tortilla chips.

Favorite memory of sharing this recipe:

This is the same recipe my mom always made for my family when I was a kid.

NOTE
This recipe makes enough for seconds or leftovers!

Makes 4 servings. Without optional ingredients, each serving contains:

Calories: 355

Fat: 7g

Sodium: 1026mg

Carbs: 47g

Sugar: 8g

Protein: 24g

· Nut-Free

White Chili

Janie Steele, Moore, OK

Prep. Time: 30 minutes ⚜ *Cooking Time: 6–8 hours* ⚜ *Ideal slow-cooker size: 3-qt.*

1 small onion, chopped

4-oz. can of chopped green chilies

2 cloves garlic, chopped, or 1 tsp. jarred minced garlic

1 tsp. cumin

2 15.8-oz. cans great northern beans, drained and rinsed

14½-oz. can chicken broth

1½ cups chopped cooked chicken

shredded cheese, sour cream, and salsa for garnish

1. Combine all ingredients in slow cooker except cheese, sour cream, and salsa.

2. Cover and cook on Low for 6–8 hours.

3. Serve with shredded cheese, sour cream, and salsa for garnish.

NOTE
This recipe makes enough for seconds or leftovers!

Makes 4 servings. Without optional toppings, each serving contains:

Calories: 357
Fat: 5g
Sodium: 650mg
Carbs: 46g
Sugar: 4g
Protein: 30g

• Gluten-Free
• Nut-Free

Chicken Taco Chili

Hope Comerford, Clinton Township, MI

Prep. Time: 15 minutes ❧ *Cooking Time: 6–7 hours* ❧ *Ideal slow-cooker size: 3-qt.*

½ cup canned black beans, drained and rinsed

½ cup canned cannellini beans, drained and rinsed

4 oz. boneless, skinless chicken breast, diced

¾ cup salsa

½ jalapeño pepper, seeded, diced

½ cup corn kernels

¼ cup chopped red onion

½ of 14½-oz. can diced tomatoes

4 oz. tomato paste

1 tsp. chili powder

1 tsp. cumin

1 tsp. salt

½ tsp. oregano

¼ tsp. pepper

4 cups gluten-free or regular chicken stock

1. Place all ingredients into the crock.

2. Cover and cook on Low for 6–7 hours.

Makes 2 servings. Each serving contains:

Calories: 305
Fat: 2.5g
Sodium: 2703mg
Carbs: 55g
Sugar: 16g
Protein: 29.5g

- Gluten-Free
- Dairy-Free
- Nut-Free

Main Dishes

Beef with Broccoli

Ne'cole Cichowlas, Chesterfield, MI

Prep. Time: 5–10 minutes 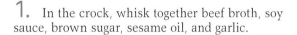 *Cooking Time: 5–6 hours, plus 30 minutes*   *Ideal slow-cooker size: 3-qt.*

14½-oz. can beef broth

½ cup low-sodium soy sauce

¼ cup brown sugar

1 Tbsp. sesame oil

3 (or more) cloves garlic, minced

1 lb. sirloin steak, sliced thin

4 Tbsp. cornstarch

¼ cup water

1 head of fresh broccoli, cored, chopped

2 cups cooked white rice

1. In the crock, whisk together beef broth, soy sauce, brown sugar, sesame oil, and garlic.

2. Add steak to crock and stir well to coat.

3. Place lid on slow cooker and cook on Low for 5–6 hours.

4. After cooking time is complete, in a small bowl mix cornstarch and water. (I like to season mine with a little pepper.) Pour over mixture in the slow cooker.

5. Add the broccoli and stir well to combine everything.

6. Return lid to the slow cooker, kick the temperature up to High, and cook for an additional 30 minutes, or until broccoli is cooked.

7. When done, serve over warm rice and enjoy.

NOTE
This recipe makes enough for seconds or leftovers!

Makes 4 servings. Each serving contains:

Calories: 464
Fat: 14.5g
Sodium: 1644mg
Carbs: 59.5g
Sugar: 20g
Protein: 32.5g

• Dairy-Free
• Nut-Free

Beef and Cabbage

Charlotte Shaffer, East Earl, PA

Prep. Time: 15 minutes ⚬ *Cooking Time: 4 hours* ⚬ *Ideal slow-cooker size: 1½-qt.*

½ lb. ground beef
1 ½ cups shredded cabbage
¾ cup barbecue sauce

1. Brown beef over medium heat.

2. Combine cabbage, beef, and sauce in slow cooker.

3. Cover. Cook on Low 4 hours.

Makes 2 servings. Each serving contains:

Calories: 234
Fat: 14g
Sodium: 1157mg
Carbs: 47.5g
Sugar: 38.5g
Protein: 22g

- Dairy-Free
- Gluten-Free
- Nut-Free

Carne Asada Nachos

Hope Comerford, Clinton Township, MI

Prep. Time: 10 minutes ⚜ *Cooking Time: 4–6 hours* ⚜ *Baking Time: 8–10 minutes* ⚜ *Ideal slow-cooker size: 2-qt.*

3/4 lb. flank steak

4 oz. gluten-free or regular beef stock

½ Tbsp. lime juice

½ tsp. smoked paprika

½ tsp. garlic powder

½ tsp. onion powder

¼ tsp. cumin

¼ tsp. chili powder

¼ tsp. salt

⅛ tsp. pepper

tortilla chips

2 tablespoons chopped onion, *optional*

¾ cup shredded cheese (of your choice)

¼ lime, wedged, *optional*

¼ cup fresh cilantro, chopped, *optional*

¼ avocado, sliced, *optional*

1. Place the flank steak into the crock.

2. Mix together the beef stock, lime juice, smoked paprika, garlic powder, onion powder, cumin, chili powder, salt, and pepper. Pour this over the steak.

3. Cover and cook on Low for 4–6 hours.

4. Remove the steak and let it rest. Slice it into thin strips.

5. Preheat your oven to 400°F.

6. On a baking sheet, spread out the chips and top them with the steak, onion (if desired), and cheese.

7. Bake for 8–10 minutes, or until the cheese is melted.

8. Before serving, if desired, squeeze the lime wedges over your nachos to taste and top with the fresh cilantro and avocado slices.

Makes 3 servings. Each serving contains:

Calories: 519
Fat: 25g
Sodium: 948mg
Carbs: 33g
Sugar: 0.5g
Protein: 33.5g

• Gluten-Free
• Nut-Free

Enchiladas

Janie Steele, Moore, OK

Prep. Time: 30 minutes & *Cooking Time: 4–6 hours* & *Ideal slow-cooker size: 2-qt.*

½ lb. ground beef, browned and drained

¼ cup chopped onion

½ of a 10½-oz. can of cheddar cheese soup

½ of a 10½-oz. can of cream of mushroom soup

½ of a 10½-oz. can of Cambell's Golden Mushroom soup

5 oz. canned enchalilada sauce (mild or hot, depending on taste)

½ of a 4-oz. can chopped chilies

6 corn tortillas

sour cream and salsa, *optional*

1. Combine all ingredients in crock except tortillas, sour cream, and salsa.

2. Cover and cook on Low for 4–6 hours.

3. One hour before serving, tear up tortillas and add to mixture.

4. Serve with sour cream and salsa, if desired.

Makes 3 servings. Without optional toppings, each serving contains:

Calories: 362
Fat: 16g
Sodium: 1568mg
Carbs: 38g
Sugar: 7g
Protein: 18.5g

• Nut-Free

Chili Burgers

Carol Eveleth, Cheyenne, WY

Prep. Time: 10 minutes ⚘ *Cooking Time: 2 hours* ⚘ *Ideal slow-cooker size: 1½-qt.*

1 lb. ground beef

1 ½ cups cornflakes crushed to ½ cup

¼ cup ketchup

1 egg, slightly beaten

2 Tbsp. onion, finely chopped

2 tsp. Worcestershire sauce

1 tsp. chili powder

1 tsp. seasoned salt

4 hamburger buns

1. Combine ground beef, cornflakes, ketchup, egg, onion, Worcestershire sauce, chili powder, and seasoned salt.

2. Shape into 4 patties.

3. Broil or grill for 2 minutes or until seared on both sides.

4. Put in crock, cover, and cook for 2 hours on Low or until desired. Serve on toasted hamburger buns with topping of choice.

NOTE
This recipe makes enough for seconds or leftovers!

Makes 4 servings. Each serving contains:

Calories: 393

Fat: 15g

Sodium: 966mg

Carbs: 38g

Sugar: 9g

Protein: 26g

• Nut-Free

Coney Dogs

Anita Troyer, Fairview, MI

Prep. Time: 30 minutes 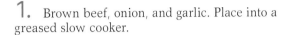 Cooking Time: 2–3 hours 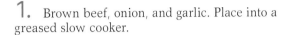 Ideal slow-cooker size: 3-qt.

¾ lb. ground beef

⅓ cup diced onion

1 clove garlic, minced

3 tsp. chili powder

2 tsp. mustard

6 oz. tomato sauce

¾ cup water

4–5 hot dogs

1. Brown beef, onion, and garlic. Place into a greased slow cooker.

2. Add rest of ingredients except hot dogs and mix well.

3. Add hot dogs on top and heat for 2–3 hours on Low.

4. Serve in hot dog buns.

NOTE
This recipe makes enough for seconds or leftovers!

Makes 4 servings. Not including buns, each serving contains:

Calories: 359

Fat: 24g

Sodium: 800mg

Carbs: 7g

Sugar: 3.5g

Protein: 22.5g

• Nut-Free

Sloppy Joes

Carol Eveleth, Cheyenne, WY

Prep. Time: 10 minutes ⚘ *Cooking Time: 3 hours* ⚘ *Ideal slow-cooker size: 3-qt.*

1 lb. ground beef, browned
¾ cup tomato juice
½ cup ketchup
½ cup quick oats
¼ cup chopped celery
1 small onion, chopped
¼ cup cream of mushroom soup
¼ cup milk
1 pkg. sloppy joe seasoning mix
½ tsp. salt

1. Mix all ingredients together and put in crock.

2. Cover and cook for 3 hours on Low.

Serving suggestion:
Serve on hamburger buns.

NOTE
This recipe makes enough for seconds or leftovers!

Makes 4 servings. Not including buns, each serving contains:

Calories: 305
Fat: 14.5g
Sodium: 1486mg
Carbs: 26g
Sugar: 14.5g
Protein: 23g

• Nut-Free

Bar-B-Que Beef

Carol Eveleth, Cheyenne, WY

Prep. Time: 10 minutes ⚬ *Cooking Time: 3 hours* ⚬ *Ideal slow-cooker size: 3-qt.*

1 lb. ground beef
¾ cup chopped celery
½ cup chopped onion
¾ cup ketchup
2 Tbsp. brown sugar
2 Tbsp. Worcestershire sauce
1 Tbsp. mustard
½ tsp. salt

1. Brown ground beef with celery and onion.

2. Place in crock along with the rest of the ingredients.

3. Cover and cook for 3 hours on Low.

Serving suggestion:
Serve over hamburger buns.

NOTE
This recipe makes enough for seconds or leftovers!

Makes 4 servings. Not including buns, each serving contains:

Calories: 325
Fat: 13g
Sodium: 2202mg
Carbs: 23g
Sugar: 9g
Protein: 20.5g

· Dairy-Free
· Gluten-Free
· Nut-Free

Poor Man's Steak

Carol Eveleth, Cheyenne, WY

Prep. Time: 15 minutes ⚶ *Cooking Time: 3–8 hours* ⚶ *Ideal slow-cooker size: 2-qt.*

1 lb. ground beef

½ cup saltine crackers, crushed

½ cup milk

1 small onion, chopped

⅛ tsp. black pepper

½ tsp. salt

¼ cup flour

10½-oz. can cream of mushroom soup

1 cup milk

1. Mix together ground beef, cracker crumbs, ½ cup milk, chopped onion, black pepper, and salt.

2. Form into patties and roll into flour to coat the patties.

3. Brown patties in well-greased pan.

4. Place patties in crock.

5. Cover patties with 1 can of mushroom soup mixed with 1 cup milk.

6. Cover and cook for 3–4 hours on High, 6–8 hours on Low.

Favorite memory of sharing this recipe:

This is a family favorite! My daughter had it served at her wedding.

NOTE
This recipe makes enough for seconds or leftovers!

Makes 4 servings. Using whole milk, each serving contains:

Calories: 380

Fat: 20g

Sodium: 1021mg

Carbs: 23g

Sugar: 6.5g

Protein: 25g

• Nut-Free

Highland Pie

Jane Geigley, Lancaster, PA

Prep. Time: 30 minutes ⚜ *Cooking Time: 2–3 hours* ⚜ *Ideal slow-cooker size: 3-qt.*

1 lb. ground beef, cooked and drained

10½-oz. can cream of mushroom soup

2 cups cooked corn

1 tsp. seasoned black pepper

3–4 cups mashed potatoes

1. Combine ground beef and mushroom soup.

2. Place in greased crock.

3. Put corn on top.

4. Sprinkle with pepper.

5. Place mashed potatoes on top of everything.

6. Cover and cook on High for 2–3 hours.

Favorite memory of sharing this recipe:

On cold winter days after working outside, my husband would love when I made this. We were two poor newlyweds, without a lot of grocery money, so this was an inexpensive and very filling meal we would often share!

NOTE
This recipe makes enough for seconds or leftovers!

Makes 4 servings. Using 3 cups mashed potatoes made with butter and whole milk, each serving contains:

Calories: 502
Fat: 23.5g
Sodium: 1098mg
Carbs: 48g
Sugar: 5g
Protein: 26g

• Nut-Free

Hamburger Meal-in-a-Crock

Jane Geigley, Lancaster, PA

Prep. Time: 30 minutes ⚶ *Cooking Time: 2 hours* ⚶ *Ideal slow-cooker size: 3-qt.*

½ lb. ground beef, browned and drained

½ cup mozzarella cheese

1 16-oz. can spaghetti sauce with mushrooms

½ lb. jumbo macaroni shells, cooked and drained

1. Mix meat, cheese, and ½ can of spaghetti sauce.

2. Fill shells with the mixture.

3. Place in greased crock.

4. Pour remaining spaghetti sauce over top.

5. Cover and cook on High for 2 hours.

Makes 3 servings. Each serving contains:

Calories: 553
Fat: 16g
Sodium: 775mg
Carbs: 74g
Sugar: 16.5g
Protein: 29.5g

• Nut-Free

Mock Ham Loaf

Carol Eveleth, Cheyenne, WY

Prep. Time: 15 minutes ☙ *Cooking Time: 3 hours* ☙ *Ideal slow-cooker size: 1½- or 2½-qt.*

½ lb. ground beef

4 oz. hot dogs, ground or chopped very fine

½ cup saltine cracker crumbs

½ beaten egg

½ tsp. salt

⅛ tsp. black pepper

¼ cup brown sugar

¼ cup tomato juice

⅛ cup water

1½ tsp. vinegar

½ tsp. mustard

1½ tsp. cornstarch

1. Mix ground beef, ground or chopped hot dogs, cracker crumbs, egg, salt, and pepper.

2. Make sauce with brown sugar, tomato juice, water, vinegar, and mustard.

3. Mix half of sauce into meat mixture.

4. Put meat mixture in crock.

5. Thicken remaining sauce with the cornstarch and pour over the meat mixture.

6. Cover and cook for 3 hours on Low.

Makes 3 servings. Each serving contains:

Calories: 368
Fat: 19.5g
Sodium: 570mg
Carbs: 33.5g
Sugar: 23g
Protein: 20g

· Nut-Free

Cheesaroni

Janeen Troyer, Fairview, MI

Prep. Time: 25 minutes ♣ Cooking Time: 2 hours, plus 25 minutes ♣ Ideal slow-cooker size: 2½-qt.

1 cup uncooked macaroni

½ lb. ground beef

½ of 10½-oz. can condensed tomato soup (do not dilute)

½ of 10½-oz. can condensed mushroom soup (do not dilute)

½ green pepper, diced

1 cup grated cheddar cheese

½ of 3-oz. can french-fried onions

onion, basil, oregano, or Italian blend

1. Cook macaroni as directed. Drain.

2. In a large skillet brown beef with your favorite seasonings.

3. Add soups, green peppers, and macaroni and mix.

4. Place half the mixture in a greased crock. Sprinkle with half of the cheese. Top with remaining mixture and cheese.

5. Cover and cook on Low for 2 hours.

6. Top with the french-fried onions, re-cover, and cook for 25 minutes longer.

TIP
This can be made with sausage.

Makes 3 servings. Each serving contains:

Calories: 510
Fat: 30g
Sodium: 943mg
Carbs: 31g
Sugar: 7g
Protein: 26g

• Nut-Free

Apple Sauce Honey Pork Chops

Maria Shevlin, Sicklerville, NJ

Prep. Time: under 30 minutes   *Cooking Time: 4 hours*   *Ideal slow-cooker size: 3-qt.*

4 boneless pork loin chops

onion powder, to taste

black pepper, to taste

¼ cup apple sauce

⅛ cup honey

1. Season both sides of the chops with onion powder and black pepper.

2. In a frying pan sear the chops on both sides.

3. Add the chops to the crock with any drippings.

4. Mix together the apple sauce and honey and then pour over the top of the chops.

5. Cover and cook on Low for 4 hours.

Serving suggestion:

Goes well with rice, asparagus, and steamed baby carrots.

Makes 2 servings. Made with 12 ounces loin end pork chops and 1 teaspoon onion powder, each serving contains:

Calories: 410

Fat: 16g

Sodium: 78mg

Carbs: 20g

Sugar: 18.5g

Protein: 46g

- Gluten-Free
- Dairy-Free
- Soy-Free
- Nut-Free

Brown Family Pork Chops

Pat Brown, Medford, NJ

Prep. Time: 10 minutes ⚜ *Cooking Time: 7–8 hours* ⚜ *Ideal slow-cooker size: 3-qt.*

4 pork chops, medium cut, with or without bone

½ cup water

1 medium onion, sliced

10 oz. canned sliced pineapple

½ cup barbecue sauce (your preference)

1. Place chops in bottom of cooker.

2. Add ½ cup of water. Cook on Low 6 hours.

3. After 6 hours, place a slice of onion and a slice of pineapple on each chop, topped with a generous scoop of barbecue sauce.

4. Cook for another hour or two on Low, or until done.

Favorite memory of sharing this recipe:

My husband graduated from Gettysburg College in Pennsylvania, 1957. This was a favorite dish in his frat house, KDR. It became our family favorite.

NOTE
This recipe makes enough for seconds or leftovers!

Makes 4 servings. Using one pound boneless loin end pork chops and juice pack pineapple, each serving contains:

Calories: 341
Fat: 11g
Sodium: 422mg
Carbs: 26.5g
Sugar: 21g
Protein: 31.5g

· Dairy-Free
· Gluten-Free
· Nut-Free

BBQ Pulled Pork Sandwiches

Hope Comerford, Clinton Township, MI

Prep. Time: 10 minutes & Cooking Time: 7 hours & Ideal slow-cooker size: 2-qt.

¾ lb. boneless pork loin

¼ cup thinly sliced sweet onion

½ cup ketchup

1 Tbsp. apple cider vinegar

2 tsp. dry mustard

1 Tbsp. brown sugar or molasses

½ tsp. onion powder

½ tsp. garlic powder

½ tsp. cumin

½ tsp. salt

¼ tsp. chili powder

gluten-free or regular buns

1. Spray crock with nonstick spray.

2. Place pork loin and onion into crock.

3. In a small bowl, mix together the ketchup, apple cider vinegar, dry mustard, brown sugar, onion powder, garlic powder, cumin, salt, and chili powder. Pour this over the contents of the crock.

4. Cover and cook on Low for 7 hours.

5. Remove the pork loin and shred it between 2 forks. Mix it back through the sauce in the crock.

6. Serve on buns.

Makes 2 servings. Not including buns, each serving contains:

Calories: 428
Fat: 16g
Sodium: 2067mg
Carbs: 26g
Sugar: 22.5g
Protein: 47g

- Gluten-Free
- Dairy-Free
- Soy-Free
- Nut-Free

Sausage, Potatoes & Green Beans

Ne'cole Cichowlas, Chesterfield, MI

Prep. Time: 5–10 minutes ☙ Cooking Time: 2–5 hours ☙ Ideal slow-cooker size: 2-qt.

6 oz. smoked sausage, sliced into pieces on an angle

2 potatoes, cubed

¼ lb. fresh green beans

7 oz. low-sodium chicken broth

½ Tbsp. butter

salt, pepper, and garlic, to taste

1. Place all ingredients in slow cooker, using the salt, pepper, and garlic to taste. Stir.

2. Cover and cook on Low 4–5 hours or High for 2–3 hours.

Favorite memory of sharing this recipe:

This is one of our favorite meals; I have experimented with many different types of sausage and loved them all. You really can't go wrong with this dish. It's a winner.

Makes 2 servings. Not including garlic, salt, and pepper, each serving contains:

Calories: 500
Fat: 32.5g
Sodium: 1224mg
Carbs: 31g
Sugar: 2g
Protein: 25.5g

• Nut-Free

Sausage and Apples

Charlotte Shaffer, East Earl, PA

Prep. Time: 10 minutes ⚬ *Cooking Time: 1 hour* ⚬ *Ideal slow-cooker size: 1½-qt.*

½ lb. smoked sausage

1 large apple, cored and sliced

⅛ cup brown sugar

¼ cup apple juice

1. Cut meat into 2-inch pieces.

2. Place all ingredients in slow cooker and mix well.

3. Cover and cook on Low 1 hour or until heated through.

Makes 2 servings. Each serving contains:

Calories: 466
Fat: 27g
Sodium: 952mg
Carbs: 33.5g
Sugar: 32g
Protein: 20.5g

- Dairy-Free
- Nut-Free

Tramp Roast for Two

Lori Stull, Rochester Hills, MI

Prep. Time: 15 minutes   ♣   Cooking Time: 4–6 hours   ♣   Ideal slow-cooker size: 3-qt.

1 cup sliced carrots

3 medium potatoes, quartered

1 onion, quartered

½ small cabbage, cut into chunks

4 cups chicken or vegetable broth

1-lb. pkg. Polish sausage or kielbasa, cut in 3 inch pieces

1. Place vegetables in the slow cooker.

2. Pour broth over vegetables.

3. Place sausage pieces on top of vegetables.

4. Cook for 4 hours on High, 6 hours on Low, or until vegetables are tender.

Favorite memory of sharing this recipe:

As a kid, my family would camp with a large group of people. We would always have a tramp roast together . . . cooking giant pots of this over the charcoal grills. It was enough to feed an army, but I always loved it so much that I make small meals of it now. The flavors blend together so well!

Makes 2 servings. Each serving contains:

Calories: 611

Fat: 23g

Sodium: 3580mg

Carbs: 65.5g

Sugar: 25.5g

Protein: 53g

- Dairy-Free
- Nut-Free

Italian Bread Pudding

Susan Kasting, Jenks, OK

Prep. Time: 20 minutes ♣ *Cooking Time: 2 hours* ♣ *Ideal slow-cooker size: 3-qt.*

1 lb. Italian sausage, cooked and crumbled

½ onion, chopped

½ large loaf of Italian bread, cubed

½ tsp. oregano

½ tsp. basil

½ tsp. garlic powder

2 chopped tomatoes

¼ cup chopped parsley

4 eggs

1 cup milk

1 cup shredded Italian cheese

1. Mix together the sausage, onion, bread, oregano, basil, garlic powder, tomatoes, and parsley in slow cooker.

2. In a bowl, mix together eggs and milk and pour over bread mixture. Let it soak in for a few minutes.

3. Cover and cook on High 2 hours. Top with cheese and cover and allow it to melt. Serve warm.

Serving Suggestion:

This is good with some marinara sauce on top.

NOTE
This recipe makes enough for seconds or leftovers!

Makes 4 servings. Each serving contains:

Calories: 686
Fat: 41g
Sodium: 992mg
Carbs: 39g
Sugar: 8.5g
Protein: 38.5g

• Nut-Free

Ham and Macaroni Dinner

Charlotte Shaffer, East Earl, PA

Prep. Time: 5 minutes   ♣   Cooking Time: 2½–3 hours   ♣   Ideal slow-cooker size: 2-qt.

1 cup shredded cheese (your choice)
1 cup macaroni, uncooked
1½ cups milk
1 can cream of mushroom soup
1½ cups of cubed cooked ham

1. Place all ingredients in slow cooker. Mix together gently until well blended.

2. Cover and cook on High 2½–3 hours, until macaroni is cooked but not overdone.

Makes 4 servings. Using cheddar cheese and whole milk, each serving contains:

Calories: 610
Fat: 34g
Sodium: 1160mg
Carbs: 39g
Sugar: 9g
Protein: 37g

• Nut-Free

Jambalaya

Ne'cole Cichowlas, Chesterfield, MI

Prep. Time: 15 minutes ⚜ *Cooking Time: 3–6 hours, plus 20–30 minutes* ⚜ *Ideal slow-cooker size: 3-qt.*

6 oz. smoked sausage, cut into rounds

½ lb. boneless, skinless chicken breast

1 stalk celery, chopped

1 clove garlic, minced

½ of a green bell pepper, chopped

2 green onions, diced

⅛ cup fresh parsley, chopped

14½-oz. can petite diced tomatoes with green chilies

1 small onion, diced

¾ cup low-sodium chicken broth

3 Tbsp. tomato paste

3 oz. tomato sauce

1 tsp. Cajun seasoning

salt and pepper, to taste

6 jumbo shrimp (I prefer precooked and frozen; just thaw before using)

2 cups cooked white or brown rice

1. Place all ingredients in slow cooker except shrimp and rice. Mix well.

2. Cook on Low 6 hours or High for 3 hours.

3. Remove chicken and shred.

4. Return shredded chicken to slow cooker.

5. Add the shrimp to the slow cooker and cook 20–30 minutes more.

6. Add rice to the slow cooker. Mix well and serve.

NOTE
This recipe makes enough for seconds or leftovers!

Makes 4 servings. Made with white rice, each serving contains:

Calories: 393
Fat: 14g
Sodium: 882mg
Carbs: 32g
Sugar: 6g
Protein: 30.5g

• Dairy-Free
• Nut-Free

Chicken, Sausage, Shrimp & Turkey Jambalaya Mamma Maria Style

Maria Shevlin, Sicklerville, NJ

Prep. Time: 30 minutes 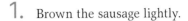 *Cooking Time: 6 hours* ❧ *Ideal slow-cooker size: 3 qt.*

½ lb. hot/sweet sausage, sliced into rings

1 cup cooked turkey or chicken breast, cut into cubes

½ medium onion, chopped

3 cloves garlic, minced

2 stalks celery, chopped

½ large red bell pepper, chopped

1 Tbsp. Cajun seasoning

1 cup spaghetti sauce

1 cup water

½ lb. small shrimp, peeled, and deveined

rice

1. Brown the sausage lightly.

2. Place into the crock along with the drippings and add the precooked turkey or chicken.

3. Toss in the onion, garlic, celery, and red bell pepper. Mix well.

4. Add in the Cajun seasoning, spaghetti sauce, and water.

5. Cover and cook on Low for 5½ hours.

6. Add in your shrimp and stir. Place lid back on immediately to retain heat and cook another 30 minutes.

7. Serve over steamed rice.

NOTE

This recipe makes enough for seconds or leftovers!

Makes 4 servings. Without rice, each serving contains:

Calories: 318
Fat: 17g
Sodium: 640mg
Carbs: 13g
Sugar: 8.5g
Protein: 24g

- Dairy-Free
- Nut-Free

One-Pot Honey Garlic Chicken Meal

Hope Comerford, Clinton Township, MI

Prep. Time: 10 minutes ♣ Cooking Time: 7 hours ♣ Ideal slow-cooker size: 3-qt.

12–14 oz. small yellow potatoes

14 oz. baby carrots

6 boneless, skinless chicken thighs

⅓ cup honey

⅓ cup gluten-free soy sauce

2 Tbsp. freshly minced garlic

¼ cup freshly minced onion

1 tsp. Italian herb blend

¼ tsp. pepper

1. Spray the crock with nonstick spray.

2. Place the yellow potatoes and carrots into the bottom of the crock and place the chicken thighs on top.

3. In a small bowl or liquid measuring cup, mix together the honey, soy sauce, minced garlic, minced onion, Italian herb blend, and pepper. Pour this mixture over the contents of the crock.

4. Cover and cook on Low for 7 hours.

NOTE
This recipe makes enough for seconds or leftovers!

Makes 4 servings. Each serving contains:

Calories: 435

Fat: 6g

Sodium: 1341mg

Carbs: 50g

Sugar: 26.5g

Protein: 33.5g

• Gluten-Free

• Dairy-Free

• Nut-Free

Chicken Teriyaki

Anita Troyer, Fairview, MI

Prep. Time: 20 minutes *Cooking Time: 3 hours, plus 30 minutes* *Ideal slow-cooker size: 2-qt.*

2 chicken breasts, diced into ½-inch cubes

¼ cup brown sugar

2½ Tbsp. unsweetened apple juice

2½ Tbsp. pineapple juice

2½ Tbsp. soy sauce

1½ Tbsp. cold water

1½ Tbsp. cornstarch

rice

1. Place meat into greased crock. Add rest of ingredients, except the water, cornstarch, and rice, and stir to mix well.

2. Heat on High for at least 3 hours, stirring every hour.

3. Before the next step, make sure the chicken is fully cooked.

4. In a small bowl add water and cornstarch. Combine with mixture in crock and stir quickly to mix.

5. Place lid back on and turn heat to Low. Heat for 30 minutes or until thickened. Serve over rice.

Makes 2 servings. Without rice, each serving contains:

Calories: 200
Fat: 1g
Sodium: 1214mg
Carbs: 41g
Sugar: 37g
Protein: 26g

- Dairy-Free
- Nut-Free

Hawaii-Style Chicken Thighs

Maria Shevlin, Sicklerville, NJ

Prep. Time: 30 minutes ⚶ *Cooking Time: 6–8 hours* ⚶ *Ideal slow-cooker size: 3-qt.*

4 chicken thighs
¼ cup brown sugar
10 oz. crushed pineapple and the juice
10½-oz. can tomato soup
1 bunch green onions, chopped
sesame seeds, *optional*

1. Wash chicken and pat dry.

2. Add chicken thighs to bottom of crock.

3. Sprinkle brown sugar over thighs.

4. Add remaining ingredients on top.

5. Cook on Low 8 hours or High for 6 hours.

Serving Suggestion:

Serve with noodles or rice and green beans.

Makes 2 servings. Each serving contains:

Calories: 695
Fat: 30.5g
Sodium: 845mg
Carbs: 79g
Sugar: 64.5g
Protein: 37.5g

• Nut-Free

Maui Chicken Crock

Elva Evers, Iowa City, IA

Prep. Time: 10–15 minutes ❧ *Cooking Time: 4–6 hours* ❧ *Ideal slow-cooker size: 1½–3-qt.*

3 boneless chicken breast halves, trimmed of skin and fat

1 Tbsp. oil

7–8 oz. chicken broth

10 oz. pineapple chunks

1 Tbsp. cider vinegar

2 Tbsp. brown sugar

2 tsp. soy sauce

½ clove garlic, minced

1½ Tbsp. cornstarch

2 Tbsp. water

1. Brown chicken in oil. Transfer chicken to slow cooker.

2. Combine remaining ingredients. Pour over chicken.

3. Cover. Cook on High 4–6 hours.

Serving Suggestion:

Serve over rice.

Makes 2 servings. Each serving contains:

Calories: 377
Fat: 14g
Sodium: 815mg
Carbs: 39.5g
Sugar: 31.5g
Protein: 39.5g

• Dairy-Free
• Nut-Free

Chicken Thighs
with Peach Mango BBQ Sauce

Maria Shevlin, Sicklerville, NJ

Prep. Time: 30 minutes ⚶ *Cooking Time: 8 hours* ⚶ *Ideal slow-cooker size: 3-qt.*

4 chicken thighs
2 tsp. salt-free lemon pepper seasoning
1 peach, peeled and diced
½ mango, peeled and diced
4 Tbsp. barbecue sauce

1. Place chicken thighs in the slow cooker.

2. Sprinkle with lemon pepper generously.

3. Add the diced peach and mango along with the sauce atop the chicken thighs.

4. Cover and cook on Low for 8 hours.

Serving Suggestion:

Serve with pasta with garlic and green onion as well as steamed broccoli with garlic.

Makes 2 servings. Each serving contains:

Calories: 546
Fat: 30.5g
Sodium: 513mg
Carbs: 35.5g
Sugar: 27.5g
Protein: 35g

· Dairy-Free
· Nut-Free

Lemon Chicken with Mushroom Sauce

Maria Shevlin, Sicklerville, NJ

Prep. Time: 30 minutes ⚶ *Cooking Time: 4 hours* ⚶ *Ideal slow-cooker size: 3-qt.*

2 boneless, skinless chicken breast halves, sliced into bite-sized pieces

1 tsp. olive oil

3 cloves garlic, chopped

2 cups fresh sliced mushrooms

½ cup chicken broth

4 Tbsp. lemon juice

1 whole lemon

1 tsp. parsley flakes

½–1 tsp. black pepper

1 tsp. garlic powder

¼ cup water

2 Tbsp. cornstarch

1. Lightly brown chicken in the olive oil.

2. Add to crock along with garlic, mushrooms, chicken broth, lemon juice, juice of one lemon, parsley flakes, black pepper, and garlic powder.

3. After squeezing the juice from the lemon, cut it up and place into the crock on top of the chicken.

4. Cover and cook on Low for 3½ hours.

5. Bump the temp to High and mix the water and cornstarch. Pour into the crock and stir. Cover, and cook another 30 minutes to thicken lightly.

Serving Suggestion:

Goes well with rice or pasta and garlic green beans.

Makes 2 servings. Each serving contains:

Calories: 187
Fat: 2.5g
Sodium: 293mg
Carbs: 15g
Sugar: 1.5g
Protein: 27g

• Dairy-Free
• Gluten-Free
• Nut-Free

Val's Oriental Chicken Thighs

Sue Smith, Saginaw, MI

Prep. Time: 10–15 minutes ❧ *Cooking Time: 3–4 hours* ❧ *Ideal slow-cooker size: 2-qt.*

½ cup soy sauce

½ Tbsp. minced garlic or 1 tsp. garlic powder

½ tsp. minced ginger or ¼ tsp. ginger powder

2 Tbsp. water

2 Tbsp. rice vinegar or regular vinegar

⅛ tsp. red pepper flakes or to taste or ⅛ tsp. cayenne pepper

1–2 dashes of white pepper

1½ Tbsp. brown sugar

4 chicken thighs (regular or boneless, skinless; your choice)

1. Mix together everything except the chicken thighs.

2. Pour the mixture into the crock.

3. Add the chicken.

4. Stir to coat the chicken with the mixture.

5. Cook on Low for 4 hours or 1 hour on High and 2–3 on Low.

Serving Suggesiton:

Serve with cooked rice.

TIP
I always use liner for easy cleanup!

Favorite memory of sharing this recipe:

This was my sister-in-law's recipe. She was of Japanese descent, growing up in Hawaii. She was not a fancy cook, but a good cook, and tried to prepare healthy food for my brother and her two sons. Since she passed away at only forty-one, I cherish this recipe and the memories of Val that come back when I prepare it.

Makes 2 servings. Using bone-in with skin chicken thighs, each serving contains:

Calories: 498
Fat: 30.5g
Sodium: 3892mg
Carbs: 18g
Sugar: 12g
Protein: 39g

• Dairy-Free
• Nut-Free

Onion & Garlic Smothered Chicken Legs

Maria Shevlin, Sicklerville, NJ

Prep. Time: 20 minutes ❧ *Cooking Time: 6–8 hours* ❧ *Ideal slow-cooker size: 3-qt.*

4 chicken legs

I medium onion, sliced

I small shallot, chopped

4 cloves garlic, chopped

I tsp. dried thyme

I tsp. dried dill

2 Tbsp. butter

1. Lightly brown the chicken legs in a pan.

2. Place into the crock.

3. Add the onion, shallot, garlic, dried thyme, and dried dill.

4. Place the butter on top.

5. Cover and cook on Low for 6–8 hours.

Serving Suggestion:

Noodles and green beans or broccoli go well with this.

NOTE
This recipe makes enough for seconds or leftovers!

Makes 4 servings. Each serving contains:

Calories: 447
Fat: 48g
Sodium: 241mg
Carbs: 10g
Sugar: 3g
Protein: 36.5g

- Gluten-Free
- Dairy-Free
- Nut-Free

Easy Parmesan Chicken

Jennifer Freed, Rockingham, VA

Prep. Time: 10 minutes ⚘ *Cooking Time: 3–7 hours, plus 15–30 minutes* ⚘ *Ideal slow-cooker size: 3-qt.*

4 oz. fresh mushrooms, sliced

I small onion, cut into thin wedges

½ Tbsp. olive oil

2 boneless, skinless chicken breasts

½ of a 26-oz. jar of pasta sauce

¼ tsp. dried basil leaves

⅛ tsp. dried oregano leaves

I bay leaf

¼ cup shredded part-skim mozzarella cheese

⅛ cup grated Parmesan cheese

Hot cooked spaghetti

1. Place mushrooms and onion in slow cooker.

2. Heat oil in large skillet over medium-high heat until hot. Lightly brown chicken on both sides. Place chicken in slow cooker. Pour pasta sauce over chicken; add herbs.

3. Cover; cook on Low 6–7 hours or on High 3 hours or until chicken is no longer pink in center. Remove and discard bay leaf.

4. Sprinkle chicken with cheeses. Cook, uncovered, on Low 15–30 minutes or until cheeses are melted. Serve over spaghetti.

Variation:

I have substituted other vegetables, such as sliced zucchini, cubed eggplant, or broccoli florets for the mushroom slices.

Makes 2 servings. Before adding spaghetti, each serving contains:

Calories: 345
Fat: 11g
Sodium: 957mg
Carbs: 26g
Sugar: 17g
Protein: 34.5g

• Nut-Free

Curry

Anita Troyer, Fairview, MI

Prep. Time: 30 minutes ⚜ *Cooking Time: 1½–2 hours* ⚜ *Ideal slow-cooker size: 3-qt.*

I lb. chicken, beef, or venison cut into
½-inch squares or ¼-inch strips

4 Tbsp. vegetable oil, *divided*

½ bay leaf

½ tsp. cumin

½ cup chopped onion

1½ tsp. ginger

1 tsp. fresh minced garlic

1 small tomato, diced

½ cup plain yogurt

Dash of hot sauce

½ tsp. salt

½ tsp. curry powder

1. Heat 2 Tbsp. oil in skillet and brown meat for 10 minutes.

2. Put into a greased crock.

3. Heat remaining 2 Tbsp. oil in skillet and add bay leaf, cumin, onion, ginger, and garlic and fry for 5 minutes, stirring every 30 seconds.

4. To skillet mixture, add tomato and fry for another minute, then remove from heat. Add yogurt, hot sauce, salt, and curry powder. Mix well.

5. Pour skillet mixture over meat in the crock. Put on Warm setting of slow cooker for 1½–2 hours. This gives time for the flavors to mix well.

Serving Suggestion:

Eat with rice or naan.

TIP
If you prefer more sauce, add some extra yogurt.

NOTE
This recipe makes enough for seconds or leftovers!

Makes 4 servings. Using chicken breast meat, each serving contains:

Calories: 291
Fat: 34g
Sodium: 439mg
Carbs: 6g
Sugar: 3g
Protein: 28g

- Gluten-Free
- Nut-Free

Main Dishes 187

Chicken Tikka Masala

Susan Kasting, Jenks, OK

Prep. Time: 15 minutes ⚜ *Cooking Time: 3–6 hours, plus 20 minutes* ⚜ *Ideal slow-cooker size: 3-qt.*

1 lb. chicken breast or boneless, skinless thighs

½ onion, chopped

2 cloves garlic, minced

1 Tbsp. grated ginger

15-oz. can pureed tomatoes

1 Tbsp. olive oil

½ Tbsp. garam masala

1 tsp. cumin

½ tsp. paprika

½ Tbsp. cayenne pepper

1 bay leaf

dash of cinnamon

½ cup Greek yogurt

¼ cup cream or Greek yogurt

1 tsp. cornstarch

1. Cut chicken into large pieces. The smaller they are the less time is needed to cook.

2. Place all ingredients in slow cooker except cream and cornstarch.

3. Cover and cook on Low for 6 hours or High for 3 hours.

4. Mix ¼ cup cream or Greek yogurt with 1 tsp. cornstarch. Add and mix into chicken and let cook for another 20 minutes to thicken.

Serving Suggestion:

Great on rice and with naan.

NOTE This recipe makes enough for seconds or leftovers!

Makes 4 servings. Using chicken breast meat, each serving contains:

Calories: 233
Fat: 13g
Sodium: 564mg
Carbs: 13g
Sugar: 7g
Protein: 31g

• Gluten-Free
• Soy-Free
• Nut-Free

Chicken Chow Mein à la Mamma Maria

Maria Shevlin, Sicklerville, NJ

Prep. Time: 30 minutes ❧ Cooking Time: 6–8 hours ❧ Ideal slow-cooker size: 3-qt.

1 boneless, skinless chicken breast, cut into cubes

2 boneless, skinless chicken thighs, cut into cubes

1 tsp. ground ginger

2–3 cloves of garlic, chopped fine

10½-oz. can fat-free chicken gravy

1¼ cup shredded carrots

6–8 mushrooms, sliced

4 ribs celery, sliced

2 onions, sliced

½ can bean sprouts

½ can sliced water chestnuts

2 sprigs green onion, chopped for garnish, *optional*

1. Season the chicken with the ginger and lightly brown in a pan with the garlic. Add the chicken, garlic, and any juices to the crock.

2. Add the canned gravy.

3. Add in the carrots, mushrooms, celery, onions, bean sprouts, and water chestnuts. Mix well.

4. Cover and cook for 6–8 hours on Low.

5. Serve with chopped green onions, if desired.

Serving Suggestion:

Serve with steamed white rice and top with some soy sauce and sesame seeds.

NOTE

This recipe makes enough for seconds or leftovers!

Makes 4 servings. Before adding rice, soy sauce, and sesame seeds, each serving contains:

Calories: 172
Fat: 2g
Sodium: 534mg
Carbs: 19g
Sugar: 5.5g
Protein: 19g

• Nut-Free

Sweet & Sour Chicken

Maria Shevlin, Sicklerville, NJ

Prep. Time: 30 minutes ⚜ *Cooking Time: 4–6 hours* ⚜ *Ideal slow-cooker size: 3-qt.*

1 lb. boneless, skinless chicken thighs, cut into 1-inch pieces.

3 cloves garlic, thinly sliced

½ small hot chili pepper, thinly sliced, *optional*

¼ each of red and green bell pepper, cubed

½ small onion, cubed

1-inch piece fresh ginger, peeled and cut into matchsticks

¼ cup apricot jam

1 cup pineapple

4 sprigs of green onion, cut into 2-inch pieces

2 Tbsp. white vinegar

1. Lightly brown chicken in a pan along with the garlic and chili pepper, if using.

2. Transfer to the crock.

3. Add in the bell peppers, onion, ginger, apricot jam, pineapple, and green onions.

4. Sprinkle on the vinegar and mix well.

5. Cover and cook on Low 4–6 hours.

Serving Suggestion:

Serve over quinoa or brown rice and with garlic green beans.

NOTE
This recipe makes enough for seconds or leftovers!

Makes 4 servings. Before adding rice or quinoa, each serving contains:

Calories: 222
Fat: 4.5 g
Sodium: 111mg
Carbs: 21g
Sugar: 17g
Protein: 22g

· Gluten-Free
· Dairy-Free
· Soy-Free
· Nut-Free

Chicken Stroganoff

Ne'cole Cichowlas, Chesterfield, MI

Prep. Time: 5 minutes ⚬ *Cooking Time: 3–6 hours* ⚬ *Ideal slow-cooker size: 3-qt.*

1½ boneless, skinless chicken breasts, cubed (about 8 oz.)

4 oz. sliced fresh mushrooms

4 oz. cream cheese, softened

10½-oz. can cream of mushroom soup

½ Tbsp. soy sauce

½ Tbsp. Worcestershire sauce

½ pkg. dry onion soup mix

1 tsp. garlic powder

salt and pepper, to taste

fresh parsley, for garnish

½ lb. large egg noodles

1. Place chicken in the bottom of the slow cooker.

2. Place mushrooms on top of chicken.

3. In medium bowl, mix together all the other ingredients except for the parsley and the noodles; pour in the slow cooker.

4. Cook on Low 4–6 hours or on High 3–4 hours.

5. Stir before serving. Place spoonfuls on top of cooked noodles and garnish with fresh parsley.

Variation:

Add a splash or two of milk or heavy cream to thin the sauce once cooked if you prefer a thinner consistency.

Makes 2 servings. Each serving contains:

Calories: 611
Fat: 29.5g
Sodium: 2253g
Carbs: 53.5g
Sugar: 5g
Protein: 44g

• Nut-Free

Yogurt Stroganoff Chicken

Jane Geigley, Lancaster, PA

Prep. Time: 15 minutes ⚜ *Cooking Time: 3 hours* ⚜ *Ideal slow-cooker size: 3-qt.*

2 Tbsp. vegetable oil

1 lb. skinless, boneless chicken breasts, cut into strips

2 cups sliced mushrooms

1 medium chopped onion

10½-oz. can condensed cream of chicken soup

1 cup plain nonfat yogurt

¼ cup water

1 lb. peas

4 cups hot-cooked noodles

sprinkle of paprika

1. In medium skillet over medium-high heat, heat oil and cook chicken until browned on all sides.

2. Pour into crock.

3. Add remaining ingredients except paprika.

4. Cover and cook for 3 hours on High.

5. Sprinkle with paprika before serving.

NOTE
This recipe makes enough for seconds or leftovers!

Makes 4 servings. Each serving contains:

Calories: 471
Fat: 8.5g
Sodium: 664mg
Carbs: 40.5g
Sugar: 11g
Protein: 46g

• Nut-Free

Chicken à la Queen

Ne'cole Cichowlas, Chesterfield, MI

Prep. Time: 5 minutes ⚜ *Cooking Time: 3–6 hours* ⚜ *Ideal slow-cooker size: 2-qt.*

1 boneless, skinless chicken breast

6 oz. frozen mixed veggies

6 oz. chicken gravy

½ of a 10½-oz. can cream of mushroom soup

½ of a 10½-oz. can cream of chicken soup

4 oz. cream cheese

¼ cup heavy cream

½ tsp. garlic powder

½ tsp. celery salt

½ Tbsp. Italian seasoning

½ of a package of egg noodles, cooked

1. Place chicken in bottom of the slow cooker.

2. In a large bowl mix all remaining ingredients together with the exception of the noodles. Once mixed together place in the crock on top of the chicken.

3. Cover and cook on Low for 6 hours or High for 3 hours.

4. Remove chicken and shred.

5. Place shredded chicken back in crock and stir well. Let sit for about 10 minutes.

6. Spoon over egg noodles and enjoy.

Makes 2 servings. Each serving contains:

Calories: 820
Fat: 45.5g
Sodium: 2476mg
Carbs: 55.5g
Sugar: 8g
Protein: 40.5g

• Nut-Free

Chicken Dumplings

Elva Evers, Iowa City, IA

Prep. Time: 30–45 minutes ⚜ *Cooking Time: 3 hours* ⚜ *Ideal slow-cooker size: 3-qt.*

2 chicken breasts

2½ cups water

⅓ cup sliced carrots

2 Tbsp. chopped onion

2 Tbsp. chopped celery

3/4 cup frozen green peas

½ cup water

2–3 Tbsp. flour

½ tsp. salt

buttermilk baking mix for dumplings

paprika, to taste

1. Cook chicken in 2½ cups water. Cool, skin, and debone chicken. Return water to boiling in pot. (May need to add water to make 2 cups of broth.)

2. Cook carrots, onions, celery in microwave on High for 5 minutes.

3. Meanwhile, combine ½ cup water and flour until smooth. Add to boiling chicken broth. Make sure gravy is fairly thick. (If broth doesn't have much flavor, add 1–2 tsp. boullion.) Season with salt.

4. Combine chicken, cooked vegetables and frozen peas, and gravy in slow cooker.

5. Mix dumplings as directed on baking mix box. Place dumplings on top of chicken in slow cooker. Sprinkle with paprika.

6. Cover. Cook on High 3 hours.

Divided into 2 portions, before adding dumplings, each portion contains:

Calories: 210

Fat: 9g

Sodium: 692mg

Carbs: 17g

Sugar: 4.5g

Protein: 31g

• Soy-Free

• Nut-Free

Chicken in a Pot

Elva Evers, Iowa City, IA

Prep. Time: 15–30 minutes ⚘ *Cooking Time: 3½–10 hours* ⚘ *Ideal slow-cooker size: 1½–3 qt.*

2 carrots, sliced

½ cup diced or sliced onion

2 celery ribs, diced

1½ cups cut-up chicken

1 tsp. salt

½ tsp. dried basil

¼ cup water (may need ½ cup if cooking on High)

1. Place vegetables in bottom of slow cooker. Place chicken on top of vegetables. Add seasonings and water.

2. Cover. Cook on Low 8–10 hours, or High 3½–5 hours.

NOTE
For a full meal add 2 medium potatoes, quartered, to vegetables before cooking.

Makes 2 servings. Using skinless chicken thigh meat, each serving contains:

Calories: 226

Fat: 6g

Sodium: 784mg

Carbs: 10.5g

Sugar: 5.5g

Protein: 31.5g

- Gluten-Free
- Dairy-Free
- Soy-Free
- Nut-Free

Chicken Meal-in-a-Crock

Jane Geigley, Lancaster, PA

Prep. Time: 30 minutes ⚮ *Cooking Time: 2 hours* ⚮ *Ideal slow-cooker size: 2-qt.*

15-oz. can of peas

10½-oz. can cream of chicken soup

1½ cups diced cooked chicken

1 tsp. pepper

1 lb. jumbo macaroni shells, cooked and drained

1½ cups milk

1. Combine peas, soup, chicken, and pepper.

2. Fill the shells with the mixture.

3. Place in greased crock.

4. Pour milk over shells.

5. Cover and cook on High for 2 hours.

NOTE
This recipe makes enough for seconds or leftovers!

Makes 4 servings. Each serving contains:

Calories: 517

Fat: 13g

Sodium: 990mg

Carbs: 108g

Sugar: 16g

Protein: 36.5g

• Nut-Free

Creamy Chicken Filling

Susan Kasting, Jenks, OK

Prep. Time: 15 minutes ⚶ *Cooking Time: 4–6 hours* ⚶ *Ideal slow-cooker size: 2-qt.*

1 ½ tsp. oil

½ tsp. cumin

½ tsp. chili powder

½ tsp. garlic powder

½ tsp. onion powder

½ tsp. salt

¼ tsp. oregano

¼ tsp. smoked paprika

½ lb. boneless, skinless chicken, cut into chunks

1 Tbsp. water

2 oz. cream cheese

¼ cup salsa

1. Mix all spices with the oil and rub on the chicken.

2. Put the water in the bottom of the crock and add chicken.

3. Cover and cook 4–6 hours on Low, depending on size of chicken pieces.

4. When cooked through, shred the chicken and add the cream cheese and salsa. Mix together.

Serving Suggestion:

This is a great filling for tacos or enchiladas.

NOTE
This recipe makes enough for seconds or leftovers!

Makes 4 servings. Not including enchilada or taco shells, each serving contains:

Calories: 126

Fat: 7g

Sodium: 189mg

Carbs: 5g

Sugar: 1g

Protein: 15g

- Gluten-Free
- Soy-Free
- Nut-Free

Chicken Verde Tostadas

Kristina Barbaza, Washington, MI

Prep. Time: 15–20 minutes ⚬ Cooking Time: 4 hours ⚬ Ideal slow-cooker size: 2½-qt.

4 3-oz. boneless, skinless chicken thighs

8 oz. salsa verde (for extra spicy, I use Herdez Guacamole Salsa)

4 tostada shells

½ avocado sliced into 8 slices

4 oz. queso fresco

¼ red onion, chopped

1 plum tomato, seeded, chopped

2 Tbsp. cilantro, chopped

1. Place chicken in slow cooker.

2. Top with the salsa verde.

3. Cover and cook on High for 4 hours.

4. Shred chicken and stir it back through the sauce in the crock.

5. Top each tostada with about 3 oz. chicken, 2 slices avocado, and 1 oz. queso fresco, and divide equally the red onion, tomato, and cilantro among the tostadas.

Favorite memory of sharing this recipe:

This was a throw-together, "let's see if it works" recipe. I actually think the salsa verde was bought because it was on sale! It was a big hit and fun to put on your own toppings and has been a favorite ever since. You can easily change the fresh toppings or add things your family likes such as cucumbers or red peppers.

NOTE
Serving size is 2 tostadas as standalone dinner, or serve one tostada with a side salad.

Makes 2 servings. Each serving contains:

Calories: 592
Fat: 42g
Sodium: 1206mg
Carbs: 31.5g
Sugar: 7g
Protein: 47.5g

• Soy-Free
• Nut-Free

Easy Chicken Taco Filling

Carrie Fritz, Meridian, ID

Prep. Time: 5 minutes ⚜ *Cooking Time: 4 hours* ⚜ *Ideal slow-cooker size: 3-qt.*

2 chicken breasts (about 8 oz.)

10-oz. can of Ro-Tel tomatoes and green chilies

15½-oz. can of black beans, drained and rinsed

1. Place chicken in a greased slow cooker.

2. Add Ro-Tel tomatoes and drained black beans over the top.

3. Cook on Low for 4 hours.

4. Shred chicken right in the slow cooker.

Serving Suggestion:

This is great to use in tortillas, on salad, or over rice. Good toppings include cheese, sour cream, lettuce, tomatoes, crushed tortilla chips, etc.

NOTE
This recipe makes enough for seconds or leftovers!

Makes 4 servings. Each serving contains:

Calories: 164
Fat: 1.5g
Sodium: 293mg
Carbs: 18g
Sugar: 1.5g
Protein: 20g

- Gluten-Free
- Dairy-Free
- Soy-Free
- Nut-Free

Tacos for Two

Michele Ruvola, Vestal, NY

Prep. Time: 10 minutes ☘ *Cooking Time: 5 hours* ☘ *Ideal slow-cooker size: 2-qt.*

2 chicken breasts

4 oz. zesty Italian dressing

¾ tsp. minced garlic

½ pkg. ranch dressing mix

¼ cup water

¼ tsp. chili powder

¼ tsp. ground cumin

taco shells

Optional toppings:

chopped jalapeños

shredded cheese

sour cream

salsa

1. Place everything but the shells and toppings in the slow cooker. Stir the ingredients a little to combine.

2. Cover and cook on Low for 5 hours.

3. Remove chicken from slow cooker when done and place on a cutting board. Shred the chicken.

4. Warm taco shells according to package directions.

5. Put chicken into taco shells, and top with favorite toppings.

Serving Suggestion:

Serve alongside a salad.

Makes 2 servings. Without taco shells and optional toppings, each serving contains:

Calories: 232
Fat: 1g
Sodium: 1163mg
Carbs: 4g
Sugar: 1g
Protein: 26g

• Nut-Free

Delectable & Easy Turkey in the Crock

Sue Smith, Saginaw, MI

Prep. Time: 10 minutes ♣ Cooking Time: 6 hours ♣ Ideal slow-cooker size: 3-qt.

1 lb. turkey breast, thawed and gravy packet removed

¼ pkg. dry onion soup mix

¼ can jellied cranberry sauce

1. Place the turkey breast in the slow cooker.

2. Add the dry soup mix and cranberry sauce. No need to stir.

3. Cook on High for 2 hours, then on Low for 4 hours or till done.

NOTE
This recipe also works well with boneless pork loin or chicken.

NOTE
This recipe makes enough for seconds or leftovers!

Favorite memory of sharing this recipe:

Our family loves turkey, and when the kids were growing up, this was so easy and less hassle than cooking a whole turkey!

Makes 4 servings. Each serving contains:

Calories: 188
Fat: 4g
Sodium: 1064mg
Carbs: 15g
Sugar: 5.5g
Protein: 22.5g

- Dairy-Free
- Gluten-Free
- Nut-Free

Santa Fe Stuffed Peppers

Maria Shevlin, Sicklerville, NJ

Prep. Time: 30 minutes ❧ Cooking Time: 4–6 hours ❧ Ideal slow-cooker size: 2–3-qt.

½ lb. lean ground turkey or ground chicken

salt, to taste

3 Tbsp. chopped onion

3 cloves of garlic, minced

¼ cup canned black beans, drained and rinsed

1–2 Tbsp. cilantro

chopped pickled jalapeño, to taste

½ cup salsa

½ tsp. cumin

¼ cup frozen corn

2 whole red bell peppers, washed, cut in half, seeds and stems removed

⅓ cup reduced-sodium, fat-free chicken broth

5 Tbsp. shredded reduced fat Monterey Jack cheese, for garnish, *optional*

1 Tbsp. green onions, for garnish, *optional*

1. In a large skillet, brown the turkey and season with salt lightly.

2. When the turkey is browned, add the onion, garlic, black beans, cilantro, pickled jalapeño pepper, salsa, and cumin.

3. Mix well and simmer, covered, for 20 minutes.

4. Remove lid and add the corn and simmer until all the liquid reduces.

5. Drain if necessary.

6. Pack the peppers with the filling.

7. Place the bell peppers in slow cooker.

8. Add the chicken stock to the bottom.

9. Cover and cook on Low 4–6 hours .

10. During the last few moments, if desired, top with cheese and green onions.

Makes 2 servings. Without optional toppings, each serving contains:

Calories: 248
Fat: 7g
Sodium: 620mg
Carbs: 25.5g
Sugar: 10g
Protein: 19.5g

• Nut-Free

Vegetarian Stuffed Peppers

Hope Comerford, Clinton Township, MI

Prep. Time: 15 minutes & Cooking Time: 5–6 hours & Ideal slow-cooker size: 3-qt.

1 cup cooked brown rice

1 cup canned black beans, drained and rinsed

½ cup chopped yellow onion

¾ cup corn kernels

¾ cup chopped tomatoes

1½ cups shredded mozzarella, *divided*

1 Tbsp. freshly minced garlic

¾ tsp. salt

½ tsp. cumin

¼ tsp. chili powder

4 bell peppers (whatever color(s) you like), tops cut off and seeded

¾ cup marinara sauce

¼ cup water

1. Spray the crock with nonstick spray.

2. In a bowl, mix together the brown rice, black beans, onion, corn, tomatoes, 1 cup of the shredded mozzarella, garlic, salt, cumin, and chili powder. Spoon this into the 4 peppers.

3. Place the peppers into the crock.

4. In a small bowl, mix together the marinara sauce and water. Pour this evenly over the peppers in the crock.

5. Cover and cook on Low for 5–6 hours. 15 minutes before serving, sprinkle the remaining ½ cup shredded mozzarella cheese on top of each pepper and re-cover the crock.

NOTE
This recipe makes enough for seconds or leftovers!

Makes 4 servings. Each serving contains:

Calories: 332

Fat: 10g

Sodium: 1064mg

Carbs: 48g

Sugar: 14.5g

Protein: 20.5g

- Gluten-Free
- Soy-Free
- Nut-Free
- Vegetarian

South-of-the-Border Macaroni & Cheese

Jennifer Freed, Rockingham, VA

Prep. Time: 20 minutes ⚶ *Cooking Time: 2 hours* ⚶ *Ideal slow-cooker size: 2-qt.*

2½ cups cooked rotini pasta

1 cup (4 oz.) cubed American cheese

6 oz. evaporated milk

½ cup shredded sharp cheddar cheese

½ of a 4-oz. can of diced green chilies, drained

1 tsp. chili powder

1 medium tomato, seeded and chopped

2½ green onions, sliced

1. Combine all ingredients except tomato and green onions in slow cooker; mix well. Cover; cook on High 2 hours, stirring twice.

2. Stir in tomato and green onions; continue cooking until hot.

Makes 2 servings. Each serving contains:

Calories: 279

Fat: 36.5g

Sodium: 1098mg

Carbs: 69.5g

Sugar: 15g

Protein: 37g

• Nut-Free
• Vegetarian

Spinach & Cheese Tortellini

Ne'cole Cichowlas, Chesterfield, MI

Prep. Time: 5 minutes ☘ *Cooking Time: 5–6 hours* ☘ *Ideal slow-cooker size: 3-qt.*

6 oz. frozen cheese tortellini

2½ oz. fresh spinach

14½-oz. can Italian-style petite diced tomatoes

2 cups vegetable broth

4 oz. of cream cheese cut into chunks

1. Place all ingredients in slow cooker.

2. Cover and cook on Low 5–6 hours.

3. Remove lid. Give it all a big stir to mix well and serve.

Makes 2 servings. Each serving contains:

Calories: 535
Fat: 25.5g
Sodium: 897mg
Carbs: 57.5g
Sugar: 7g
Protein: 18.5g

- Nut-Free
- Vegetarian

Salmon Puff

Jane Geigley, Lancaster, PA

Prep. Time: 10 minutes ❧ Cooking Time: 2–3 hours ❧ Ideal slow-cooker size: 3-qt.

½ of 1 lb. box of saltine crackers, broken

16-oz. can salmon

2½ Tbsp. butter cut into 1-inch squares

1½ cups milk

1. Place half of the broken crackers in the bottom of a greased slow cooker.

2. Pour the salmon over top.

3. Top with remaining crackers.

4. Place cut butter squares across the top.

5. Pour milk over the layers.

6. Cover and cook on High for 2–3 hours.

NOTE
This recipe makes enough for seconds or leftovers!

Makes 4 servings. Each serving contains:

Calories: 407
Fat: 18g
Sodium: 772mg
Carbs: 28.5g
Sugar: 5g
Protein: 30.5g

• Soy-Free
• Nut-Free

Atlanta Tuna Loaf

Jane Geigley, Lancaster, PA

Prep. Time: 15 minutes ❧ *Cooking Time: 3 hours* ❧ *Ideal slow-cooker size: 3-qt.*

1 cup flaked tuna

1 ½ cups bread crumbs

½ egg (beat egg and then divide in half)

1 ½ tsp. minced fresh parsley

½ tsp. salt

¼ cup chopped celery

½ small onion, chopped

⅛ tsp. pepper

½ of 10 ½-oz. can of cream of chicken soup

1. Mix all ingredients except the soup.

2. Shape into a loaf.

3. Place in a greased crock.

4. Pour soup over loaf.

5. Cover and cook on High for 3 hours.

Makes 3 servings. Each serving contains:

Calories: 382
Fat: 10g
Sodium: 949mg
Carbs: 43g
Sugar: 5g
Protein: 23g

• Nut-Free

Side Dishes & Vegetables

Cheesy Broccoli & Cauliflower

Hope Comerford, Clinton Township, MI

Prep. Time: 15 minutes   Cooking Time: 2½–3½ hours, plus 10 minutes   Ideal slow-cooker size: 2-qt.

2 eggs

I Tbsp. cornstarch

I cup shredded cheddar cheese, *divided*

¼ cup cottage cheese

¼ tsp. salt

¼ tsp. onion powder

¼ tsp. garlic powder

⅛ tsp. pepper

¾ cup chopped cauliflower florets

¾ cup chopped broccoli florets

¼ cup chopped onion

1. Spray crock with nonstick spray.

2. In a bowl, mix together the eggs, cornstarch, ¾ cup of the shredded cheddar cheese, cottage cheese, salt, onion powder, garlic powder, and pepper.

3. Stir the cauliflower, broccoli, and onion into the cheese mixture. Pour this into the crock.

4. Cover and cook on Low for 2½–3½ hours.

5. Sprinkle the remaining ¼ cup of shredded cheddar cheese over the top of the contents of the crock 10 minutes before serving and re-cover.

NOTE
This recipe makes enough for seconds or leftovers!

Makes 4 servings. Each serving contains:

Calories: 176

Fat: 12.5g

Sodium: 420mg

Carbs: 13g

Sugar: 6g

Protein: 1.5g

- Gluten-Free
- Soy-Free
- Nut-Free
- Vegetarian

Carrots for Two

Hope Comerford, Clinton Township, MI

Prep. Time: 10 minutes ⚬ Cooking Time: 3–4 hours ⚬ Ideal slow-cooker size: 2-qt.

6 carrots, peeled, sliced into ½-inch thick rounds

3 Tbsp. water

1 tsp. coconut sugar

1 Tbsp. butter

dash of salt

¼ cup fresh chopped parsley

1. Spray crock with nonstick spray.

2. Combine carrots, water, coconut sugar, butter, and salt in crock.

3. Cover and cook on Low for 3–4 hours.

4. Before serving, toss the carrots with the parsley.

Makes 2 servings. Each serving contains:

Calories: 135
Fat: 5.5g
Sodium: 172mg
Carbs: 25.5g
Sugar: 12g
Protein: 3g

- Gluten-Free
- Soy-Free
- Nut-Free
- Vegetarian

Orange Carrots

Hope Comerford, Clinton Township, MI

Prep. Time: 5 minutes ⚬ *Cooking Time: 3–4 hours* ⚬ *Ideal slow-cooker size: 1½-qt.*

8–10 oz. baby carrots
2 Tbsp. orange juice
1 Tbsp. orange marmalade
⅛ tsp. salt

1. Spray crock with nonstick spray.

2. Combine all ingredients in crock.

3. Cover and cook on Low for 3–4 hours.

Makes 2 servings. Each serving contains:

Calories: 193	• Gluten-Free
Fat: 0g	• Dairy-Free
Sodium: 270mg	• Soy-Free
Carbs: 23g	• Nut-Free
Sugar: 16g	• Vegetarian
Protein: 2.5g	• Vegan

Summer Veggie Medley

Hope Comerford, Clinton Township, MI

Prep. Time: 15 minutes ⚬ *Cooking Time: 2½–3 hours* ⚬ *Ideal slow-cooker size: 2-qt.*

½ cup chopped zucchini

1 cup fresh or frozen green beans, cut into ¾-inch pieces

½ cup chopped tomatoes

¼ cup diced onion

1 clove garlic, minced

2 Tbsp. olive oil

¼ cup water

1 tsp. butter

1 tsp. balsamic vinegar

¼ tsp. salt

¼ tsp. oregano

⅛ tsp. pepper

1. Spray crock with nonstick spray.

2. Combine all ingredients in crock.

3. Cover and cook on Low for 2½–3 hours.

Makes 2 servings. Each serving contains:

Calories: 123
Fat: 9g
Sodium: 26mg
Carbs: 8g
Sugar: 3.5g
Protein: 2g

- Gluten-Free
- Soy-Free
- Nut-Free
- Vegetarian

Side Dishes & Vegetables 237

Barbecue-Worthy Green Beans

Hope Comerford, Clinton Township, MI

Prep. Time: 15 minutes ॰ Cooking Time: 3–4 hours ॰ Ideal slow-cooker size: 2-qt.

½ lb. frozen or fresh green beans, cut into 1-inch pieces

¼ cup chopped onion

¼ cup ketchup

3 Tbsp. brown sugar

1 tsp. dry mustard

¼ tsp. salt

⅛ tsp. pepper

1–2 strips bacon, cooked, diced

1. Spray crock with nonstick spray.

2. Combine all ingredients in crock.

3. Cover and cook on Low for 3–4 hours.

Makes 2 servings. Each serving contains:

Calories: 173
Fat: 1.5g
Sodium: 422 mg
Carbs: 41g
Sugar: 34g
Protein: 4g

• Gluten-Free
• Nut-Free

Easy Greek Green Beans

Hope Comerford, Clinton Township, MI

Prep. Time: 5 minutes ⚓ Cooking Time: 3–4 hours ⚓ Ideal slow-cooker size: 2-qt.

½ lb. frozen or fresh green beans cut into 1-inch pieces

⅓ cup gluten-free or regular Greek salad dressing

¼ cup diced tomatoes

2 Tbsp. diced onion

1 Tbsp. crumbled feta cheese

4 pitted Kalamata olives, chopped

1. Combine green beans, Greek salad dressing, tomatoes, and onion in crock.

2. Cover and cook on Low for 3–4 hours.

3. Stir in the crumbled feta and Kalamata olives before serving.

Makes 2 servings. Each serving contains:

Calories: 283
Fat: 10g
Sodium: 286mg
Carbs: 32g
Sugar: 20.5g
Protein: 13g

· Gluten-Free
· Nut-Free
· Vegetarian

Corn-on-the-Cob

Hope Comerford, Clinton Township, MI

Prep. Time: 5 minutes ⚜ *Cooking Time: 2–3 hours* ⚜ *Ideal slow-cooker size: 3-qt.*

2 ears of corn (in the husk)

½ cup water

1. Place the ears of corn in the crock and pour in the water.

2. Cover and cook on Low for 2–3 hours.

Each ear of corn contains:

Calories: 60
Fat: 0g
Sodium: 3mg
Carbs: 14g
Sugar: 2g
Protein: 2g

- Gluten-Free
- Dairy-Free
- Soy-Free
- Nut-Free
- Vegetarian
- Vegan

Simple Cabbage

Hope Comerford, Clinton Township, MI

Prep. Time: 15 minutes ⚘ *Cooking Time: 4–5 hours* ⚘ *Ideal slow-cooker size: 2-qt.*

½ small head of green cabbage, cored, chopped very coarsely

2 slices bacon, cooked, diced

2 cups pearl onions

½ tsp. salt

¼ tsp. pepper

½ cup of gluten-free or regular chicken or vegetable stock

1. Place the cabbage, bacon, and pearl onions in the crock and mix them up.

2. Season the contents of the crock with the salt and pepper. Pour in the stock.

3. Cover and cook on Low for 4–5 hours.

Makes 2 servings. Each serving contains:

Calories: 121
Fat: 2.5g
Sodium: 896mg
Carbs: 17g
Sugar: 9g
Protein: 4g

• Gluten-Free
• Dairy-Free
• Soy-Free
• Nut-Free

Barbecued Beans

Carol Eveleth, Cheyenne, WY

Prep. Time: 10 minutes   *Cooking Time: 3 hours*   *Ideal slow-cooker size: 3-qt.*

1 lb. ground beef, browned
12-oz. can pork and beans
½ cup chopped onion
½ cup ketchup
2 Tbsp. molasses
1 Tbsp. vinegar
1 Tbsp. Worcestershire sauce

1. Mix all ingredients together in crock.

2. Cover and cook for 3 hours on Low.

NOTE
This recipe makes enough for seconds or leftovers!

Makes 4 servings. Each serving contains:

Calories: 155
Fat: 14g
Sodium: 790mg
Carbs: 36g
Sugar: 15.5g
Protein: 23g

• Nut-Free

Slow Cooker Baked Beans

Anita Troyer, Fairview, MI

Prep. Time: 30 minutes ⚗ *Cooking Time: 3 hours* ⚗ *Ideal slow-cooker size: 3-qt.*

½ lb. ground beef

¼ cup diced onion

1 clove garlic, minced

6 slices bacon

16-oz. can Bush's Baked Beans

1 cup kidney beans, drained and rinsed

1 Tbsp. molasses

¼ tsp. chili powder

2 Tbsp. ketchup

¼ cup barbecue sauce

1 Tbsp. prepared mustard

¼ cup brown sugar

1. Brown beef, onion, and garlic. Place into large mixing bowl.

2. Fry the bacon and drain. Crumble into the bowl.

3. Add the rest of the ingredients and mix well.

4. Put into a greased crock and cook on High for 3 hours.

NOTE
This recipe makes enough for seconds or leftovers!

Makes 4 servings. Each serving contains:

Calories: 448

Fat: 10g

Sodium: 1163mg

Carbs: 68g

Sugar: 41g

Protein: 15g

• Gluten-Free

• Nut-Free

Mexican-Style Pinto Beans

Hope Comerford, Clinton Township, MI

Soaking Time: 12 hours ⚬ *Prep. Time: 10 minutes* ⚬ *Cooking Time: 5 hours* ⚬ *Ideal slow-cooker size: 3-qt.*

6 oz. dry pinto beans

water

1 tomato, diced

1 jalapeño, seeded, diced

¼ cup chopped onion

2 cloves garlic, minced

1½ slices bacon, cooked, diced

½ tsp. salt

5 oz. gluten-free or regular beer

1. Place pinto beans in a bowl or pot and add enough water to cover 2 inches over the beans. Soak at least 12 hours, then drain and rinse them.

2. Place the beans into the crock with all the remaining ingredients.

3. Cover and cook on Low for 5 hours.

TIP
The beer can be replaced with any type of stock or broth you have on hand.

NOTE
This recipe makes enough for seconds or leftovers!

Makes 4 servings. Each serving contains:

Calories: 186
Fat: 1g
Sodium: 328mg
Carbs: 30.5g
Sugar: 3g
Protein: 10g

• Gluten-Free
• Dairy-Free
• Nut-Free

Healthy Barley and Lentil Pilaf

Carrie Fritz, Meridian, ID

Prep. Time: 5 minutes ❦ *Cooking Time: 3–5 hours* ❦ *Ideal slow-cooker size: 3-qt.*

⅓ cup pearl barley
⅓ cup green lentils
1 Tbsp. butter
1 Tbsp. dried onion flakes
½ tsp. dried minced garlic
2 tsp. chicken bouillon
1 bay leaf
⅛ tsp. black pepper
1⅓ cup water

1. Add all ingredients to your slow cooker and stir.

2. Cook on Low 3–5 hours.

3. Stir and serve.

Favorite memory of sharing this recipe:
This is one of my daughter's favorite dishes! She even likes to take the leftovers in her lunch box to school.

Makes 2 servings. Each serving contains:

Calories: 252
Fat: 6.5g
Sodium: 733 mg
Carbs: 39.5g
Sugar: 2g
Protein: 9g

• Nut-Free

Potato Cauliflower Mash

Hope Comerford, Clinton Township, MI

Prep. Time: 10 minutes ⚭ *Cooking Time: 6 hours, plus 10 minutes* ⚭ *Ideal slow-cooker size: 2-qt.*

10 oz. Yukon Gold potatoes, cubed

¼ cup gluten-free or regular vegetable broth

¼ head cauliflower, chopped

I Tbsp. milk

I Tbsp. butter

I Tbsp. sour cream

½ tsp. salt

½ tsp. dried dill

¼ tsp. garlic powder

¼ tsp. onion powder

⅛ tsp. pepper

1. Place potatoes and vegetable broth in crock.

2. Cover and cook on Low for 3 hours.

3. Add the cauliflower to the crock, cover, and continue cooking for an additional 3 hours.

4. At the end of cooking time, stir in the milk, butter, sour cream, salt, dill, garlic powder, onion powder, and pepper. Mash with a potato smasher or immersion blender.

5. Cover and let cook an additional 10 minutes, or until everything is heated through again.

Makes 2 servings. Each serving contains:

Calories: 249
Fat: 5.5g
Sodium: 667mg
Carbs: 41.5g
Sugar: 4g
Protein: 6g

- Gluten-Free
- Vegetarian
- Nut-Free

Sour Cream Potatoes

Janeen Troyer, Fairview, MI

Prep. Time: 25 minutes ⚭ *Cooking Time: 2 hours* ⚭ *Ideal slow-cooker size: 3-qt.*

1 small onion

2 Tbsp. butter

1 lb. shredded potatoes

10-oz. can mushroom soup

1 cup shredded cheese

1 cup sour cream

1. Chop the onion and brown in the butter.

2. In a bowl, mix together the onion, butter, potatoes, soup, cheese, and sour cream.

3. Put in a greased crock.

4. Cover and cook on Low for 2 hours. Stir every 30 minutes while cooking.

Serving Suggestion:

Goes well served with ham and green beans.

TIP

You can mix up these ingredients and freeze them to cook later. Just be sure it is thawed before putting it in the slow cooker.

NOTE

This recipe makes enough for seconds or leftovers!

Makes 4 servings. Each serving contains:

Calories: 426

Fat: 30.5g

Sodium: 790mg

Carbs: 29g

Sugar: 5g

Protein: 19g

• Nut-Free

• Vegetarian

Luck o' the Irish Boats

MarJanita Geigley, Lancaster, PA

Prep. Time: 30 minutes ♣ Cooking Time: 4–5 hours ♣ Ideal slow-cooker size: 2-qt.

2 large potatoes, washed and cut in half lengthwise

1 Tbsp. butter

½ tsp. salt

¼ tsp. pepper

¼ cup milk

½ lb. ground beef, browned and drained

½ small onion, chopped

3 bacon strips, cooked and crumbled

½ cup sour cream

¼ cup shredded cheese

3–4 rinsed clover leaves, for garnish

1. Place potatoes in slow cooker.

2. Cook for 2 hours on Low.

3. Scoop out pulp from the potatoes (leave ¼ inch in shells).

4. Mash pulp with remaining ingredients except cheese and clovers.

5. Spoon mixture into potatoes and allow to liberally top each potato.

6. Top each potato with cheese.

7. Cook potatoes for another 2–3 hours.

8. Garnish each potato half with a clover.

Makes 2 servings. Each serving contains:

Calories: 520
Fat: 38g
Sodium: 923mg
Carbs: 44g
Sugar: 3g
Protein: 32.5g

- Gluten-Free
- Nut-Free

Loaded "Baked" Potato Wedges

Hope Comerford, Clinton Township, MI

Prep. Time: 20 minutes ⚭ *Cooking Time: 7–8 hours* ⚭ *Ideal slow-cooker size: 3-qt.*

1½ lbs. red potatoes, cut into wedges

½ cup shredded cheddar cheese

2 slices bacon, cooked, chopped

¼ cup chopped yellow onion

½ Tbsp. olive oil

1 tsp. salt

½ tsp. dried dill

½ tsp. onion powder

½ tsp. garlic powder

½ tsp. dried parsley

¼ tsp. pepper

1–2 Tbsp. chopped green onions, for garnish

1. Line the crock with aluminum foil, leaving enough at the top so that you can close it up into a packet with all the ingredients inside. Spray it with nonstick spray.

2. Place the potatoes, cheddar cheese, bacon, onion, olive oil, salt, dried dill, onion powder, garlic powder, dried parsley, and pepper into the foil packet you created. Stir to coat everything evenly, then close up the foil packet at the top.

3. Cover and cook on Low for 7–8 hours.

4. Serve with freshly chopped green onions on top.

NOTE
This recipe makes enough for seconds or leftovers!

Makes 4 servings. Each serving contains:

Calories: 418

Fat: 7g

Sodium: 712mg

Carbs: 31g

Sugar: 1.5g

Protein: 7g

- Gluten-Free
- Soy-Free
- Nut-Free

Cheesy Red Potatoes

Karrie Molina, Freeland, MI

Prep. Time: 20 min. ❧ *Cooking Time: 4 hours* ❧ *Ideal slow-cooker size: 2-qt.*

1 lb. red potatoes, cut into small chunks or wedges

¼ cup chopped onion or ¼ tsp. onion salt

½ tsp. oregano

salt and pepper, to taste

1 Tbsp. butter (cut into chunks)

¼ cup grated Parmesan cheese

1. Place potatoes in slow cooker.

2. Add onion, oregano, salt, pepper, and butter.

3. Cover and cook on High for 4 hours.

4. Sprinkle with cheese as you serve.

Favorite memory of sharing this recipe:

My husband is a "meat and potatoes" kind of guy and we always seem to have extra red potatoes for quick side dishes—so this is one of our favorites.

Makes 2 servings. Each serving contains:

Calories: 266
Fat: 7.5g
Sodium: 483mg
Carbs: 41g
Sugar: 2.5g
Protein: 8.5g

- Gluten-Free
- Soy-Free
- Nut-Free
- Vegetarian

Jack's Potato Pot

Sue Smith, Saginaw, MI

Prep. Time: 20 mins. ⚜ *Cooking Time: 6 hours* ⚜ *Ideal slow-cooker size: 2-qt.*

½ of a 12oz. can evaporated milk

½ of a 10½-oz. can condensed cream of celery soup

3 strips bacon, fried and diced

12 oz. frozen hash browns

¼ onion, diced

¼ lb. Velveeta cheese, diced

1. Combine the milk, undiluted soup, bacon, hash browns, and onion in crock, then sprinkle the cheese over the top.

2. Cover and cook on Low for 6 hours.

Makes 3 servings. Each serving contains:

Calories: 344

Fat: 15g

Sodium: 1030mg

Carbs: 30g

Sugar: 10g

Protein: 13g

• Nut-Free

• Vegetarian

Sweety Sweet Potatoes

Karrie Molina, Freeland, MI

Prep. Time: 20 minutes ⚜ Cooking Time: 4–7 hours ⚜ Ideal slow-cooker size: 2-qt.

1 lb. sweet potatoes, peeled, cut into pieces

pinch of salt

¼ tsp. ground nutmeg

¾ tsp. cinnamon

2 Tbsp. dark brown sugar (packed firmly)

½ tsp. vanilla extract

1 Tbsp. butter

1. Place and mix potatoes, salt, nutmeg, cinnamon, and brown sugar in slow cooker.

2. Cover and cook on Low for 7 hours, or on High for 4 hours.

3. Add vanilla and butter.

4. Stir to blend or use hand blender to smooth.

Favorite memory of sharing this recipe:

We love this recipe in the fall but is an excellent side dish year round. It helps with our sweet tooth as well.

NOTE
This recipe makes enough for seconds or leftovers!

Makes 4 servings. Each serving contains:

Calories: 145
Fat: 3g
Sodium: 155mg
Carbs: 31g
Sugar: 13g
Protein: 2g

- Gluten-Free
- Soy-Free
- Nut-Free
- Vegetarian

Happy Yams

Hope Comerford, Clinton Township, MI

Prep. Time: 15 minutes   Cooking Time: 4 hours   Ideal slow-cooker size: 2-qt.

2 yams, peeled, chopped into bite-sized chunks

1 apple, peeled, cored, chopped

2 Tbsp. apple juice

1 tsp. lemon juice

2 Tbsp butter, melted

½ tsp. cinnamon

1. Spray crock with nonstick spray.

2. Combine all ingredients in crock.

3. Cover and cook on Low for 4 hours.

Makes 2 servings. Each serving contains:

Calories: 260
Fat: 11g
Sodium: 154mg
Carbs: 39g
Sugar: 10g
Protein: 2g

- Gluten-Free
- Soy-Free
- Nut-Free
- Vegetarian

Wild Rice with Cranberries

Hope Comerford, Clinton Township, MI

Prep. Time: 5 minutes ❧ *Cooking Time: 3½–4 hours* ❧ *Ideal slow-cooker size: 2-qt.*

¾ cup uncooked wild rice

¼ cup diced onions

¼ cup dried cranberries

½ tsp. salt

⅛ tsp. pepper

7 oz. gluten-free or regular vegetable stock

1. Combine all ingredients in crock.

2. Cover and cook on Low for 3½–4 hours.

Serving Suggestion:

Sprinkle with walnuts (unless you want the recipe to be nut-free) and chopped fresh parsley.

Makes 2 servings. Each serving contains:

Calories: 338
Fat: 1.5g
Sodium: 377mg
Carbs: 72g
Sugar: 15g
Protein: 10g

- Gluten-Free
- Dairy-Free
- Nut-Free (optional)
- Vegetarian

Cheesy Rice

Hope Comerford, Clinton Township, MI

Prep. Time: 5 minutes ⚕ *Cooking Time: 3–4 hours, plus 10 minutes* ⚕ *Ideal slow-cooker size: 2-qt.*

¾ cup uncooked brown rice

2 Tbsp. diced onion

1 Tbsp. butter

¼ tsp. salt

⅛ tsp. pepper

2¼ cups gluten-free or regular vegetable stock

¾ cup shredded cheddar cheese

1. Combine brown rice, diced onion, butter, salt, pepper, and stock in crock.

2. Cover and cook on Low for 3–4 hours.

3. Stir the cheese through the rice, cover, and cook an additional 10 minutes.

Makes 2 servings. Each serving contains:

Calories: 326
Fat: 21g
Sodium: 449mg
Carbs: 57g
Sugar: 0.5g
Protein: 16.5g

• Gluten-Free
• Nut-Free
• Vegetarian

Desserts & Beverages

Blueberry Torte

Jane Geigley, Lancaster, PA

Prep. Time: 30 minutes ⚜ *Cooking Time: 2–3 hours* ⚜ *Ideal slow-cooker size: 2-qt.*

6 crushed graham crackers

2 Tbsp. butter, melted

⅜ cup sugar, *divided*

4 oz. cream cheese, softened

1 egg

½ can of blueberry pie filling

1. Mix graham crackers, butter, and half of sugar.

2. Press mixture into crock.

3. Mix cream cheese, rest of sugar, and egg until smooth.

4. Spread on top of graham crackers.

5. Pour blueberry filling over top.

6. Cover and cook on High for 2–3 hours.

Serving Suggestion:

Serve warm with vanilla ice cream.

NOTE
This recipe makes enough for seconds or leftovers!

Makes 3 servings. Each serving contains:

Calories: 395
Fat: 23.5g
Sodium: 337mg
Carbs: 71g
Sugar: 51g
Protein: 5g

• Soy-Free
• Nut-Free
• Vegetarian

Strawberry Cobbler

Karrie Molina, Freeland, MI

Prep. Time: 10 min.   ❧   Cooking Time: 1½–4 hours   ❧   Ideal slow-cooker size: 2-qt.

½ of a 21-oz. can of strawberry pie filling (or cherry if you prefer)

½ of a box yellow cake mix

4 Tbsp. butter, melted

1. Place the pie filling at the bottom of the slow cooker.

2. Mix the cake and butter in a separate bowl.

3. Sprinkle over pie filling (do not mix).

4. Cover and cook on Low for 3–4 hours, or High for 1½–2 hours.

Serving Suggestion:

You can place ice cream alongside or whipped topping on individual servings.

Favorite memory of sharing this recipe:

My husband and I enjoy this because it reminds us of pie without all the extra effort. We have enjoyed it over vanilla ice cream and with whipped topping on top.

NOTE
This recipe makes enough for seconds or leftovers!

Makes 4 servings. Before adding topping, each serving contains:

Calories: 396
Fat: 15.5g
Sodium: 502mg
Carbs: 61.5g
Sugar: 40g
Protein: 1g

• Soy-Free
• Nut-Free
• Vegetarian

No-Sugar-Added Cherry Cobbler

Janie Steele, Moore, OK

Prep. Time: 20 minutes   *Cooking Time: 1–2 hours*   *Ideal slow-cooker size: 2-qt.*

20-oz. can no-sugar-added cherry pie filling (can use other flavors)

1 cup flour

¼ cup melted butter

½ cup skim milk

1 ½ tsp. baking powder

½ tsp. almond extract

¼ tsp. salt

ice cream or whipped topping, *optional*

1. Grease crock.

2. Combine all but optional ingredients, reserving a little of the cherry pie filling to pour over the top just before serving the cobbler. Mix until smooth.

3. Cover and cook for 1–2 hours, or until heated through.

4. Serve with ice cream or whipped topping, if desired.

NOTE
This recipe makes enough for seconds or leftovers!

Makes 4 servings. Before adding topping, each serving contains:

Calories: 279

Fat: 11g

Sodium: 442mg

Carbs: 25g

Sugar: 8g

Protein: 5g

- Soy-Free
- Vegetarian

Munchy Rhubarby Crunch

Jane Geigley, Lancaster, PA

Prep. Time: 30 minutes ⚜ Cooking Time: 2–3 hours ⚜ Ideal slow-cooker size: 2-qt.

½ cup sifted flour

⅜ cup uncooked oatmeal

½ cup brown sugar

4 Tbsp. butter, melted

½ tsp. cinnamon

2 cups diced rhubarb

½ cup sugar

I Tbsp. cornstarch

½ cup water

½ tsp. vanilla extract

1. Mix flour, oatmeal, brown sugar, butter, and cinnamon to make crumbs.

2. Press half of the crumbs into greased crock.

3. Layer rhubarb over top.

4. Mix sugar, cornstarch, water, and vanilla in small pan and cook until thick and clear (constantly stirring).

5. Pour over rhubarb.

6. Top with remaining crumbs.

7. Cover and cook on High for 2–3 hours.

Makes 3 servings. Each serving contains:

Calories: 515

Fat: 15g

Sodium: 112mg

Carbs: 114g

Sugar: 86g

Protein: 4.5g

• Soy-Free

• Nut-Free

• Vegetarian

Amazing Caramel Apple Crunch

Hope Comerford, Clinton Township, MI

Prep. Time: 20 minutes ⚜ *Cooking Time: 4 hours* ⚜ *Cooling Time: 1 hour* ⚜ *Ideal slow-cooker size: 2-qt.*

½ cup brown sugar

¼ cup turbinado sugar

2–3 Honeycrisp apples, cut into bite-sized chunks

½ tsp. cinnamon

½ tsp. vanilla extract

½ tsp. cornstarch

dash of nutmeg

⅛ tsp. salt

Crumble:

⅓ cup gluten-free or regular old-fashioned oats

⅓ cup brown sugar

2 Tbsp. almond flour

¼ tsp. cinnamon

1½ Tbsp. coconut oil, in solid but softened form, or butter

1. Spray crock with nonstick spray.

2. Mix the brown sugar and turbinado sugar together and spread it across the bottom of the crock.

3. Toss the apples with the cinnamon, vanilla, cornstarch, nutmeg, and salt. Pour evenly over the sugar mix at the bottom of the crock.

4. Mix the crumble ingredients together in a bowl with your fingers. Sprinkle this over the apples.

5. Cover and cook on Low for 4 hours. Let sit to cool for 1 more hour, with the cover off, before serving. This will allow the caramel to thicken.

Serving Suggestion:

Serve over your favorite vanilla ice cream, or delicious vanilla Greek yogurt.

NOTE
This recipe makes enough for seconds or leftovers!

Makes 4 servings. Without toppings, each serving contains:

Calories: 333
Fat: 7g
Sodium: 73mg
Carbs: 83.5g
Sugar: 74g
Protein: 2g

- Gluten-Free
- Dairy-Free
- Soy-Free
- Vegetarian
- Vegan

Chocolate Cherry Cheesecake Crumble

Sue Hamilton, Benson, AZ

Prep. Time: 10 minutes ⚶ *Cooking Time: 1½ hours* ⚶ *Ideal slow-cooker size: 2-qt.*

15-oz. can of dark sweet cherries with juice

3.4-oz. box of cheesecake instant pudding mix

12 double-stuff chocolate sandwich cookies, broken (I just use my hands)

4 Tbsp. butter, melted

1. Spray the crock with nonstick spray.

2. Pour the cherries in the crock. Add 4 tablespoons of the instant pudding and stir it in.

3. In a bowl, combine the broken cookies and the butter. Stir until well mixed.

4. Add the rest of the dry pudding mix to the cookie mixture. Spoon the mixture evenly on top of the fruit.

5. Cover and cook on High for 1½ hours.

Serving Suggestion:

Serve warm with whipped cream.

NOTE
This recipe makes enough for seconds or leftovers!

Makes 4 servings. Before adding whipped cream, each serving contains:

Calories: 506
Fat: 21.5g
Sodium: 635mg
Carbs: 76g
Sugar: 61.5g
Protein: 1g

- Soy-Free
- Nut-Free
- Vegetarian

Apple Caramel Oatmeal Cream Betty

Sue Hamilton, Benson, AZ

Prep. Time: 10 minutes ❧ *Cooking Time: 1½ hours* ❧ *Ideal slow-cooker size: 2-qt.*

3 cups peeled and sliced apples

3.4-oz. box caramel instant pudding mix

4 oatmeal cream pie soft sandwich cookies, broken

4 Tbsp. butter

1 egg, beaten, or 4 Tbsp. egg substitute

1. Spray the crock with nonstick spray.

2. Combine the apples with 4 tablespoons of the instant pudding and stir it in.

3. In a bowl, combine the broken cookies and the butter. Stir until well mixed.

4. Add the rest of the dry pudding mix to the cookie mixture. Mix well.

5. Add the egg, stirring until well blended. Spoon the mixture evenly on top of the fruit.

6. Cover and cook on High for 1½ hours.

Serving Suggestion:

Serve warm with whipped cream.

NOTE
This recipe makes enough for seconds or leftovers!

Makes 4 servings. Without whipped cream, each serving contains:

Calories: 392
Fat: 17.5g
Sodium: 535mg
Carbs: 56.5g
Sugar: 43.5g
Protein: 3.5g

• Nut-Free
• Vegetarian

Peach Pecan Delight

Sue Hamilton, Benson, AZ

Prep. Time: 10 minutes ☙ Cooking Time: 1½ hours ☙ Ideal slow-cooker size: 2-qt.

15-oz. can sliced peaches with the juice

3.4-oz. box instant vanilla pudding mix, divided

12 pecan shortbread cookies, broken (I just use my hands to do this)

4 Tbsp. butter, melted

1. Spray the crock with nonstick spray.

2. Pour the peaches into the crock. Add 4 tablespoons of the instant pudding and stir it in.

3. In a bowl, combine the broken cookies and the butter. Stir until well mixed.

4. Add the rest of the dry pudding mix to the cookie mixture. Spoon the mixture evenly on top of the fruit.

5. Cover and cook on High for 1½ hours.

Serving Suggestion:

Serve warm with whipped cream.

NOTE
This recipe makes enough for seconds or leftovers!

Makes 4 servings. Without whipped cream, each serving contains:

Calories: 501
Fat: 26g
Sodium: 697mg
Carbs: 62g
Sugar: 45g
Protein: 4g

• Vegetarian

Amish Shoo-Fly Melt

MarJanita Geigley, Lancaster, PA

Prep. Time: 30 minutes ⚜ *Cooking Time: 2–3 hours* ⚜ *Ideal slow-cooker size: 2-qt.*

½ baked 9-inch pie shell broken into crumbles

½ cup flour

⅜ cup brown sugar

2¼ tsp. shortening

½ tsp. baking soda

½ cup boiling water

½ cup molasses

½ beaten egg

1. Place pie crumbles in bottom of greased crock.

2. Mix flour, sugar, and shortening until crumbly.

3. Set ¼ cup of the mixture aside.

4. Dissolve the baking soda in the water.

5. Add the crumbs to molasses, egg, and baking soda mix, keeping the ¼ cup aside.

6. Place in crock.

7. Sprinkle the reserved crumbs over top.

8. Cook on high for 2–3 hours.

Makes 3 servings. Each serving contains:

Calories: 471
Fat: 10g
Sodium: 361mg
Carbs: 100g
Sugar: 69g
Protein: 4.5g

- Nut-Free
- Vegetarian

Peanut Butter and White Chocolate Macadamia Nut Cake

Andrea Maher, Dunedin, FL

Prep. Time: 10 minutes ⚜ *Cooking Time: 3 hours* ⚜ *Ideal slow-cooker size: 3–4-qt.*

¼ cup coconut oil

¼ cup coconut sugar

⅓ cup powdered peanut butter

3 Tbsp. gluten-free or regular oat flour

2 large eggs, beaten

½ tsp. vanilla extract

sea salt, to taste

2 Tbsp. white chocolate chips

2 Tbsp. cup crushed macadamia nuts

2 tsp. white chocolate chips for topping, *optional*

2 tsp. crushed macadamia nuts for topping, *optional*

1. Line the crock with a large piece of foil; spray with nonstick spray.

2. Whisk all ingredients together except the chips and nuts for topping.

3. Place a piece of paper towel over the top of the slow cooker and secure with the lid. Cook on Low for 3 hours; the cake should be set around the edges and gooey in the center.

4. Serve warm in a pretty bowl. Sprinkle 1 Tbsp. white chocolate chips and 1 Tbsp. crushed macadamia nuts on top, if desired.

Makes 3 servings. Without optional toppings, each serving contains:

Calories: 386

Fat: 29g

Sodium: 359mg

Carbs: 30.5g

Sugar: 19g

Protein: 10g

- Gluten-Free
- Vegetarian

Gooey Chocolate Cake For Two

Andrea Maher, Dunedin, FL

Prep. Time: 10 minutes   ❧   Cooking Time: 3 hours   ❧   Ideal slow-cooker size: 3–5-qt.

½ cup unsweetened applesauce

½ cup coconut sugar

⅔ cup unsweetened cocoa

⅓ cup gluten-free or regular oat flour

3 large eggs, beaten

1 tsp. vanilla extract

sea salt, to taste

½ cup chocolate chips

2 Tbsp. peanut butter, melted, *optional*

1. Line the crock with a large piece of foil, spray with nonstick spray.

2. Whisk all ingredients together except the melted peanut butter.

3. Place a piece of paper towel across the top of the slow cooker, secure with the lid, and cook on Low for 3 hours; the cake should be set around the edges and gooey in the center.

4. Serve warm and in a pretty bowl. Drizzle some melted peanut butter on top if you desire.

Makes 2 servings. Without peanut butter, each serving contains:

Calories: 609
Fat: 21.5g
Sodium: 822mg
Carbs: 110.5g
Sugar: 63.5g
Protein: 20.5g

- Gluten-Free
- Nut-Free
- Vegetarian

Chocolate Obsession in a Slow Cooker

Sue Smith, Saginaw, MI

Prep. Time: 15 minutes ❧ Cooking Time: 2 hours ❧ Ideal slow-cooker size: 3-qt.

1¾ cups light brown sugar, *divided*

1 cup flour

¼ cup plus 3 Tbsp. cocoa powder, *divided*

2 tsp. baking powder

¼ tsp. salt

½ cup milk

2 Tbsp. butter, melted

½ tsp. vanilla extract

¼ tsp. almond extract

1¾ cup hot water

vanilla ice cream

1. Stir together 1 cup brown sugar, flour, 3 Tbsp. cocoa powder, baking powder, and salt.

2. Whisk in the milk, butter, vanilla extract, and almond extract.

3. Spread into the slow cooker.

4. Mix the rest of the brown sugar and cocoa.

5. Sprinkle over the batter.

6. Pour in the hot water, but do not stir.

7. Cover and cook for 2 hours on High.

8. Test with a toothpick in the center; it should come out clean.

9. Spoon into dishes and serve with ice cream.

NOTE
This recipe makes enough for seconds or leftovers!

Makes 4 servings. Without ice cream, each serving contains:

Calories: 517

Fat: 8g

Sodium: 444mg

Carbs: 143g

Sugar: 114g

Protein: 7.5g

- Soy-Free
- Vegetarian

White Chocolate Coconut Dream Bar

Andrea Maher, Dunedin, FL

Prep. Time: 15 minutes ❧ Cooking Time: 3 hours ❧ Ideal slow-cooker size: 3–5-qt.

2 large eggs, separated

¼ cup coconut sugar

½ tsp. vanilla extract

¼ cup melted coconut oil

½ cup organic unsweetened gluten-free or regular shredded coconut

½ cup gluten-free or regular oats

1 cup full-fat organic coconut milk

2 Tbsp. white chocolate chips

1. Spray your crock with nonstick spray.

2. Beat the egg whites with a hand mixer on high for 2–3 minutes until stiff peaks form.

3. In a separate bowl, beat the yolks with the sugar. Add the vanilla extract, coconut oil, coconut, and oats until thoroughly combined.

4. Slowly add the coconut milk. Gently fold in the egg whites until combined.

5. Pour the mixture into your crock.

6. Place paper towels over the top of the slow cooker opening and secure with the lid.

7. Cook on Low for 2–3 hours.

8. Top with the white chocolate chips and add a little extra shredded coconut, if desired.

NOTE
This recipe makes enough for seconds or leftovers!

Makes 4 servings. Each serving contains:

Calories: 451
Fat: 37.5g
Sodium: 82mg
Carbs: 27g
Sugar: 15.5g
Protein: 7g

- Gluten-Free
- Nut-Free
- Vegetarian

Orange and Peppermint Fudge

Hope Comerford, Clinton Township, MI

Prep. Time: 5 minutes ∿ Cooking Time: 2 hours ∿ Cooling Time: 4 hours ∿ Ideal slow-cooker size: 2-qt.

¾ cups semisweet chocolate chips

3.5 oz. (¼ of 14 oz. can) sweetened condensed milk

¼ tsp. vanilla extract

1 drop orange essential oil (be sure it's food-grade) or ¼ tsp. orange extract

1 drop peppermint essential oil (be sure it's food-grade) or ¼ tsp. peppermint extract

1. Spray your crock with nonstick spray.

2. Place the chocolate chips, sweetened condensed milk, and vanilla into the crock.

3. Cover and cook on Low for about 2 hours, stirring every 30 minutes.

4. Line a 4x4-inch brownie pan with parchment paper, or spray with nonstick spray.

5. When the chocolate is completely liquid, add the orange and peppermint essential oils, or extracts. Stir.

6. Pour the chocolate into the brownie pan and spread it out evenly.

7. Cover and refrigerate for 4 hours before serving.

NOTE
This recipe makes enough for seconds or leftovers!

Makes 4 servings. Each serving contains:

Calories: 264
Fat: 12g
Sodium: 45mg
Carbs: 38g
Sugar: 35.5g
Protein: 4g

- Gluten-Free
- Nut-Free
- Vegetarian

Pumpkin Pie Pudding

Janie Steele, Moore, OK

Prep. Time: 20 minutes ☙ *Cooking Time: 3 hours* ☙ *Ideal slow-cooker size: 2-qt.*

15-oz. can pumpkin

12-oz. can evaporated skim milk

¾ cup granulated Splenda®

½ cup buttermilk baking mix

2 eggs, beaten

2 tsp. pumpkin pie spice

1 tsp. lemon zest

whipped topping, *optional*

1. Combine all ingredients except whipped topping. Mix until smooth.

2. Cover and cook on Low for 3 hours.

3. Serve with whipped topping, if desired.

NOTE
This recipe makes enough for seconds or leftovers!

Makes 4 servings. Without whipped cream, each serving contains:

Calories: 254
Fat: 6g
Sodium: 488mg
Carbs: 23g
Sugar: 7g
Protein: 12.5g

- Nut-Free
- Vegetarian

Vanilla Caramel Dip

Hope Comerford, Clinton Township, MI

Prep. Time: 5 minutes ⚹ *Cooking Time: 45 minutes–1 hour* ⚹ *Ideal slow-cooker size: 1½-qt.*

13 unwrapped gluten-free or regular caramels

1 oz. plus 1 tsp. heavy cream

1 tsp. vanilla extract

apples, for dipping

1. Spray crock with nonstick spray.

2. Combine caramels, heavy cream, and vanilla in crock.

3. Cover and cook on Low for 45 minutes to 1 hour, or until completely melted.

4. Serve with apple slices for dipping.

Makes 4 servings. Without apple slices, each serving contains:

Calories: 335
Fat: 20g
Sodium: 177mg
Carbs: 55g
Sugar: 47g
Protein: 3.5g

- Gluten-Free
- Nut-Free
- Vegetarian

Spicy Milk Steamer

Anita Troyer, Fairview, MI

Prep. Time: 10 minutes   Cooking Time: 1 hour   Ideal slow-cooker size: 3-qt.

4 cups milk

¼ cup brown sugar

1 tsp. cinnamon

½ tsp. nutmeg

½ tsp. cloves

1. Add all ingredients to the crock and stir to mix well.

2. Heat on Low for 1 hour, watching to make sure it doesn't get too hot.

3. Serve in mugs and may garnish with cinnamon sticks.

NOTE
This recipe makes enough for seconds or leftovers!

Makes 4 servings. Using whole milk, each serving contains:

Calories: 191

Fat: 8g

Sodium: 98mg

Carbs: 27g

Sugar: 29g

Protein: 8g

- Gluten-Free
- Soy-Free
- Vegetarian
- Nut-Free

Vanilla Cream Coffee

Anita Troyer, Fairview, MI

Prep. Time: 8 minutes ❧ *Cooking Time: 2–2½ hours* ❧ *Ideal slow-cooker size: 3-qt.*

3 cups milk

1 cup water

¾ cup heavy cream

3 tsp. instant coffee

3 Tbsp. vanilla syrup

1. Add all ingredients to crock and stir to mix well.

2. Heat on Low for 2–2½ hours.

3. Serve in mugs.

Serving Suggestion:

Top mug with whipped topping as a garnish.

NOTE
This recipe makes enough for seconds or leftovers!

Makes 4 servings. Without whipped cream, each serving contains:

Calories: 289

Fat: 24g

Sodium: 92mg

Carbs: 15g

Sugar: 16g

Protein: 6g

- Gluten-Free
- Soy-Free
- Nut-Free
- Vegetarian

Mississippi Iced Tea

MarJanita Geigley, Lancaster, PA

Prep. Time: 15 minutes ⚜ *Cooking Time: 2 hours* ⚜ *Ideal slow-cooker size: 3-qt.*

3 black tea bags

4 cups water

½ cup sugar

1. Place water and tea bags in crock.

2. Cook on High for two hours.

3. Pour in glass pitcher and mix in sugar.

4. Refrigerate and serve over ice cubes with a sprig of fresh mint.

NOTE
This recipe makes enough for seconds or leftovers!

Makes 4 servings. Each serving contains:

Calories: 90	• Gluten-Free
Fat: 0g	• Dairy-Free
Sodium: 0mg	• Soy-Free
Carbs: 64g	• Nut-Free
Sugar: 64g	• Vegetarian
Protein: 0g	• Vegan

Winter Juice

MarJanita Geigley, Lancaster, PA

Prep. Time: 15 minutes ⚗ *Cooking Time: 3 hours* ⚗ *Ideal slow-cooker size: 3-qt.*

1 qt. water
1 cup fresh cranberries
1 cup apple cider
¼ cup orange juice
¼ cup sugar
¼ cup lemon juice
½ pack mulling spices

1. Combine all ingredients into crock.

2. Mix thoroughly.

3. Cover and cook for 3 hours on Low.

4. Strain the mulling spices out of the juice.

5. Serve warm as a tea or refrigerate and serve as an afternoon spritzer.

NOTE
This recipe makes enough for seconds or leftovers!

Makes 4 servings. Each serving contains:

Calories: 199	• Gluten-Free
Fat: 0g	• Dairy-Free
Sodium: 5mg	• Soy-Free
Carbs: 29.5g	• Nut-Free
Sugar: 26.5g	• Vegetarian
Protein: 0g	• Vegan

Metric Equivalent Measurements

If you're accustomed to using metric measurements, I don't want you to be inconvenienced by the imperial measurements I use in this book.

Use this handy chart, too, to figure out the size of the slow cooker you'll need for each recipe.

Weight (Dry Ingredients)

1 oz		30 g
4 oz	¼ lb	120 g
8 oz	½ lb	240 g
12 oz	¾ lb	360 g
16 oz	1 lb	480 g
32 oz	2 lb	960 g

Slow Cooker Sizes

1-quart	0.96 l
2-quart	1.92 l
3-quart	2.88 l
4-quart	3.84 l
5-quart	4.80 l
6-quart	5.76 l
7-quart	6.72 l
8-quart	7.68 l

Volume (Liquid Ingredients)

½ tsp.		2 ml
1 tsp.		5 ml
1 Tbsp.	½ fl oz	15 ml
2 Tbsp.	1 fl oz	30 ml
¼ cup	2 fl oz	60 ml
⅓ cup	3 fl oz	80 ml
½ cup	4 fl oz	120 ml
⅔ cup	5 fl oz	160 ml
¾ cup	6 fl oz	180 ml
1 cup	8 fl oz	240 ml
1 pt	16 fl oz	480 ml
1 qt	32 fl oz	960 ml

Length

¼ in	6 mm
½ in	13 mm
¾ in	19 mm
1 in	25 mm
6 in	15 cm
12 in	30 cm

Special Diet Index

Recipe and Ingredient Index

Equivalent Measurements

dash = little less than ⅛ tsp.

3 tsp. = 1 Tbsp.

2 Tbsp. = 1 oz.

4 Tbsp. = ¼ cup

5 Tbsp. plus 1 tsp. = ⅓ cup

8 Tbsp. = ½ cup

12 Tbsp. = ¾ cup

16 Tbsp. = 1 cup

1 cup = 8 oz. liquid

2 cups = 1 pt.

4 cups = 1 qt.

4 qt. = 1 gal.

1 stick butter = ¼ lb.

1 stick butter = ½ cup

1 stick butter = 8 Tbsp.

beans, 1 lb. dried = 2–2½ cups (depending on the size of the beans)

bell pepper, 1 large = 1 cup chopped

cheese, hard (for example, cheddar, Swiss, Monterey Jack, mozzarella), 1 lb. grated = 4 cups

cheese, cottage, 1 lb. = 2 cups

chocolate chips, 6-oz. pkg. = 1 scant cup

crackers (butter, saltines, snack), 20 single crackers = 1 cup crumbs

herbs, 1 Tbsp. fresh = 1 tsp. dried

lemon, 1 medium-sized = 2–3 Tbsp. juice

lemon, 1 medium-sized = 2–3 tsp. grated rind

mustard, 1 Tbsp. prepared = 1 tsp. dry or ground mustard

oatmeal, 1 lb. dry = about 5 cups dry

onion, 1 medium-sized = ½ cup chopped

Pasta

macaroni, penne, and other small or tubular shapes, 1 lb. dry = 4 cups uncooked

noodles, 1 lb. dry = 6 cups uncooked

spaghetti, linguine, fettucine, 1 lb. dry = 4 cups uncooked

potatoes, white, 1 lb. = 3 medium-sized potatoes = 2 cups mashed

Potatoes, sweet, 1 lb. = 3 medium-sized potatoes = 2 cups mashed

rice, 1 lb. dry = 2 cups uncooked

sugar, confectioners', 1 lb. = 3½ cups sifted

whipping cream, 1 cup unwhipped = 2 cups whipped

whipped topping, 8-oz. container = 3 cups

yeast, dry, 1 envelope (¼ oz.) = 1 Tbsp.

Assumptions about Ingredients

flour = unbleached or white, and all-purpose

oatmeal or oats = dry, quick or rolled (old-fashioned), unless specified

pepper = black, finely ground

rice = regular, long-grain (not instant unless specified)

salt = table salt

shortening = solid, not liquid

sugar = granulated sugar (not brown and not confectioners')

Substitute Ingredients

For 1 cup buttermilk—use 1 cup plain yogurt; or pour $1^1/_3$ Tbsp. lemon juice or vinegar into a 1-cup measure. Fill the cup with milk. Stir and let stand for 5 minutes. Stir again before using.

For 1 oz. unsweetened baking chocolate—stir together 3 Tbsp. unsweetened cocoa powder and 1 Tbsp. butter, softened.

For 1 Tbsp. cornstarch—use 2 Tbsp. all-purpose flour; or 4 tsp. instant tapioca.

For 1 garlic clove—use ¼ tsp. garlic salt (reduce salt in recipe by $^1/_8$ tsp.); or $^1/_8$ tsp. garlic powder.

For 1 Tbsp. fresh herbs—use 1 tsp. dried herbs.

For 8 oz. fresh mushrooms—use 1 4-oz. can mushrooms, drained.

For 1 Tbsp. prepared mustard—use 1 tsp. dry or ground mustard.

For 1 medium-sized fresh onion—use 2 Tbsp. minced dried onion; or 2 tsp. onion salt (reduce salt in recipe by 1 tsp.); or 1 tsp. onion powder. Note: These substitutions will work for meatballs and meatloaf, but not for sautéing.

For 1 cup sour milk—use 1 cup plain yogurt; or pour 1 Tbsp. lemon juice or vinegar into a 1-cup measure. Fill with milk. Stir and then let stand for 5 minutes. Stir again before using.

For 2 Tbsp. tapioca—use 3 Tbsp. all-purpose flour.

For 1 cup canned tomatoes—use $1^1/_3$ cups diced fresh tomatoes, cooked gently for 10 minutes.

For 1 Tbsp. tomato paste—use 1 Tbsp. ketchup.

For 1 Tbsp. vinegar—use 1 Tbsp. lemon juice.

For 1 cup heavy cream—add $^3/_4$ cup melted butter to ¾ cup milk. Note: This will work for baking and cooking, but not for whipping.

For 1 cup whipping cream—chill thoroughly $^2/_3$ cup evaporated milk, plus the bowl and beaters, then whip; or use 2 cups store-bought whipped topping.

For ½ cup wine—pour 2 Tbsp. wine vinegar into a ½-cup measure. Fill with broth (chicken, beef, or vegetable). Stir and then let stand for 5 minutes. Stir again before using.

About the Author

Hope Comerford is a mom, wife, elementary music teacher, blogger, recipe developer, public speaker, ALM Zone Fitness Motivator, Young Living Essential Oils essential oil enthusiast/educator, and published author. In 2013, she was diagnosed with a severe gluten intolerance and since then has spent many hours creating easy, practical, and delicious gluten-free recipes that can be enjoyed by both those who are affected by gluten and those who are not.

Growing up, Hope spent many hours in the kitchen with her Meme (grandmother), and her love for cooking grew from there. While working on her master's degree when her daughter was young, Hope turned to her slow cookers for some salvation and sanity. It was from there she began truly experimenting with recipes and quickly learned she had the ability to get a little more creative in the kitchen and develop her own recipes.

In 2010, Hope started her blog, *A Busy Mom's Slow Cooker Adventures*, simply to share the recipes she was making with her family and friends. She never imagined people all over the world would begin visiting her page and sharing her recipes with others as well. In 2013, Hope self-published her first cookbook, *Slow Cooker Recipes: 10 Ingredients or Less and Gluten-Free* and then later wrote *The Gluten-Free Slow Cooker*.

Hope is thrilled to be working with Fix-It and Forget-It and representing such an iconic line of cookbooks. She is excited to bring her creativeness to the Fix-It and Forget-It brand. Through Fix-It and Forget-It, Hope has written *Fix-It and Forget-It Lazy & Slow, Fix-It and Forget-It Healthy Slow Cooker Cookbook, Fix-It and Forget-It Favorite Slow Cooker Recipes for Mom, Fix-It and Forget-It Favorite Slow Cooker Recipes for Dad, Fix-It and Enjoy-It Welcome Home Cookbook*, and *Fix-It and Forget-It Holiday Favorites*.

Hope lives in the city of Clinton Township, Michigan, near Metro Detroit, and is a Michigan native. She has been happily married to her husband and best friend, Justin, since 2008. Together they have two children, Ella and Gavin, who are her motivation, inspiration, and heart. In her spare time, Hope enjoys traveling, singing, cooking, reading books, spending time with friends and family, and relaxing.

FIX-IT and FORGET-IT®